W9-CCA-728

A PASSION FOR GOLF

A PASSION FOR GOLF

TREASURES AND TRADITIONS OF THE GAME

By Laurence Sheehan
Photographs by William Stites
with Carol Sama Sheehan
and Kathryn George

Foreword by Arnold Palmer

Design by Paul Hardy

Clarkson Potter/Publishers
New York

Copyright © 1994 by Laurence
Sheehan, Carol Sheehan, William
Stites, and Kathryn George

Foreword copyright © 1994 by
Arnold Palmer

All rights reserved. No part of this
book may be reproduced or trans-
mitted in any form or by any means,
electronic or mechanical, including
photocopying, recording, or by any
information storage and retrieval
system, without permission in writing
from the publisher.

Published by Clarkson Potter/
Publishers, 201 East 50th Street, New
York, New York 10022. Member of
the Crown Publishing Group.

Random House, Inc. New York,
Toronto, London, Sydney, Auckland

CLARKSON N. POTTER,
POTTER, and colophon are trade-
marks of Clarkson N. Potter, Inc.

Manufactured in China

Library of Congress Cataloging-in-
Publication Data

Sheehan, Laurence.
A passion for golf: treasures and
traditions of the game / By Laurence
Sheehan; photographs by William
Stites; with Carol Sama Sheehan and
Kathryn George.
1. Golf—History. 2. Golf courses—
History. 3. Sheehan, Laurence.
I. Sheehan, Carol Sama. II. George,
Kathryn. III. Title.
GV963.S54   1994
796.352—dc20
[796.352] 93-42355

ISBN 0-517-59363-7

10 9 8 7 6 5 4 3 2 1

First Edition

CONTENTS

ACKNOWLEDGMENTS

A *Passion for Golf* could not have happened without the help and encouragement of a lot of passionate golfers. We are grateful to all the people who threw open the doors of their clubs and homes to us and who shared their proud and affectionate recollections and observations about the game with us, as well as their unique collections.

For our productive and deeply satisfying sojourn in Scotland, we have many to thank, among them:

Michael Bonallack, secretary of the R & A, for allowing us into St. Andrews's sanctum sanctorum; T. B. "Tom" Forrester, administration secretary, now retired, for helping us make the most of the rich opportunities for photography; and various unnamed members and stewards who were unfailing in their courtesy to us and enthusiasm for our project.

Peter Lewis, curator of the award-winning British Golf Museum, an American who has a knack for pinpointing the universal nature of the Scottish game.

Archie Baird, retired Edinburgh veterinarian and amateur golf historian, for an informative tour of the "Heritage of Golf" museum in Gullane, and his kindness, along with that of his wife, Sheila (great-granddaughter of Willie Park!), in receiving us in their house for tea and the contemplation of the many artistic renditions of golf the couple have collected.

Ronnie MacAskill, golf professional and general manager of the Royal Aberdeen Golf Club, and Mrs. J. J. MacNaughton, captain of the Aberdeen Ladies' Golf Club, for letting us prowl on their wild links and visit their storied club rooms.

John Simpson, secretary of Blairgowrie Golf Club in Perthshire, for allowing us a good look at an exceptional parkland course.

Gordon and Sheila McPherson of the Laurels in Blairgowrie, our host and hostess for the week, who by sheer force of their natural optimism gave us to think we were on to a good thing every time we made our dawn departure and every time we came back for supper, long after dark.

As the first country in Continental Europe to embrace the game of golf, France was a significant destination for us. We are grateful for the friendly reception we received, as *explorateurs du golf*, wherever we went. Special thanks to:

Jean-Pierre Desbrosses, for sharing the historic traditions of Golf de St.-Germain with us, as well as a bottle of champagne from his personal wine cellar.

François Kerjean, for introducing us to the wonderful style and ambience of Golf de St.-Cloud.

Dan Pesant, of the fabulous Golf de St.-Nom, for the patience to allow one of our number to say his piece in pigeon-French before revealing he, as a native of Quebec, could speak English quite as well as French.

Pierre Pouchain, for giving us the chance to see Chantilly on a day when, technically, it was closed and he and his family had better things to do.

Jean-Edouard Dulout, for welcoming us to Morfontaine, a golf course as seductive as a painting

by Monet—and for taking the time to drive us all over the course in his Peugeot station wagon!

Dominique Destrenau, who gave us a warm welcome at Le Golf National, and then made sure we stayed warm while visiting this championship layout by loaning us a couple of her windbreakers.

Above all, we would like to thank Bernard Morel and John Walker of Air France, and Bernard Cartier, of the Federation Française du Golf, for their assistance in planning our trip to France and helping us make the most of the limited time we had available to locate and document the most authentic golf traditions of this zealous sporting nation.

Our travels in North America took us to both famous and virtually unknown golfing milieus, and we owe thanks to many for allowing us that privilege, most notably: Bill Harmon at Newport CC; Karen Bednarski and her staff at the USGA; Bob Burdett of the Golf Collectors Society, and the members of East Lake CC; Jim Barclay, for putting us on the trail of Niagara-on-the-Lake, where Barbara Ahluwalia, Curtis Labelle, and Reg Rutter extended their welcome; Dorothy

Brown, of the BC Golf House; Dick Garrard of Foxburg CC; Lin and Gib Vincent, who introduced us to Arthur R. H. Clarke of Otsego GC; Jack and Peg Dezieck; Rusty and Roswitha Mott; Mr. and Mrs. Harvey Penick, for graciously receiving us in their home, and Tinsley Penick and his staff at Austin CC; Dow Finsterwald, Jr., Robert Guth, and Dennis Roberson of Colonial CC; Johnny R. Henry; Gil McNally and the heritage-minded members of Garden City GC; Lowell M. Schulman and Tom Julius; Bill Tenney at Northfield GC; Rick Pohle at Taconic GC; Wayne and Claudia Aaron of Atlanta, who gave us carte blanche in attempting to capture the depth and quality of their collection in pictures; all the good folks at Latrobe CC, especially Arnold Palmer, Jerry Palmer, and Doc Giffin; Alastair Johnston, whose own golf book, a labor of love, dwarfs these efforts; all the people who made our visit to Pinehurst so rewarding, including Dick Taylor, Wayne and Jo Ashby, Sue Love at the Tufts library, Ken Crow, and Dick Stranahan; Mike Hurdzan and David Whelchel; and to Gary and Ione Wiren, for mak-

ing us feel at home.

Thanks also to Ken and Jean Bowden, Cal Brown, Ross Goodner, and Nick Seitz for sharing some of their vast knowledge of golf's enduring traditions and values.

Other individuals who volunteered their help and encouragement along the way were April Ehrenman, Joanne Casullo, Dick Coop, Geoffrey and Carol Cornish, Larry Dornisch of Lost Tree Club, Paul Fullmer of the American Society of Golf Course Architects, Randy Jones, Jim and Ellie McCaffrey, Jim Peace, Maury Povich, and Jim Walker of Stockbridge CC.

Friends and fellow golfers who read the manuscript and provided helpful advice were Charles Adams, Bob Bagg, Tracy Kidder, and Dick and Susan Todd.

Thanks again to our agent, Gayle Benderoff.

The complex job of producing such a book was made a lot easier by having friendly and talented staffers at Clarkson Potter to work with, including Howard Klein, Renato Stanisic, Tina Constable, Nancy Maloney, Mark McCauslin, and Joan Denman. Finally, we thank Paul Hardy for a great design, and Lauren Shakely, our editor, for her steadfast support and friendship.

FOREWORD

I had the good fortune to grow up schooled in the great traditions and values of golf, in a modest frame house next to the fifth hole at Latrobe Country Club. My dad, Milfred "Deacon" Palmer, served Latrobe as greenkeeper and golf pro for more than half a century. By word and by example, he instilled in me from my earliest years a respect for the qualities that mold a virtuous golfer—sportsmanship, integrity, courtesy, competitiveness, self-reliance, appreciation for tradition, and an honest work ethic.

Pap got me started in the fundamentals when I was three by cutting down a set of battered old clubs to suit my height, and then teaching me the overlapping grip before I'd ever been corrupted by handling a baseball bat in the ten-finger style. Pap was a strict but fair taskmaster who taught me not just how to swing ("Always hit it hard"), but also the profoundly important discipline of playing the game to the best of my ability—to always do everything as hard and as well as I could.

Teachers, players, clubmakers, rulesmakers, architects, historians, collectors—the game's enthusiastic citizenry—are all found in *A Passion for Golf*, as are some of the most magical golfing venues of the world, such as St. Andrews and Royal Aberdeen, St.-Cloud and Morfontaine, Newport and Garden City, Pinehurst and Colonial, and, it gives me great pleasure to note, my own Latrobe, where the Palmer family still carries on in a style in which we think "Deacon" would approve.

As you probably know, I am a strong believer in maintaining the traditional character of golf. It's one of the things I stress in my role as national chairman of the members program for the United States Golf Association, especially now, as 1995 and the USGA's centennial year approaches.

Those of us immersed in golf sometimes forget to follow Walter Hagen's admonition "to smell the flowers," to enjoy the rich natural beauty where our game unfolds; or to appreciate the creature comforts and camaraderie offered by our clubs, public and private, famous and unknown; or to respond to the wonderful sentiments expressed in the art, crafts, trophies, clubhouse architecture, collections, and customs that golf has inspired over the years.

A Passion for Golf reminds us how lucky we are to be part of "the old game," as it salutes and celebrates a unique sporting heritage, with beautiful images that capture its eternal appeal.

I'm old-fashioned about golf, and I hope you are, too. And if you are, I think you'll thoroughly enjoy *A Passion for Golf*.

Arnold Palmer
Youngstown, Pennsylvania

INTRODUCTION

Goff, and the Man, I sing, who em'lous, plies
The jointed club; whose balls invade the skies . . .

— THOMAS MATHISON, 1743

It is late March in the hills of western Massachusetts where I make my home, and there are at least two and a half feet of snow on the ground.

But all is well. I am staring at images of the Royal and Ancient Golf Club of St. Andrews, Scotland, collected on a trip we made to the Kingdom of Fife at the peak of spring, when the gorse was ablaze in the fields between links and sea, where this classic game first took hold.

I remember vividly the first time I played the Old Course in the company of a local tradesman and his young son, and the bottle he pulled from his bag on the 18th tee, and the swig he offered me from that bottle, and the ball I subsequently drove into the road alongside the famed finishing hole. He himself ended up in the Valley of Sin, the notorious swale in front of the home green, and took a 7 or 8. I managed to beat him with an amazing 6 when I sunk a 30-footer. His lad with the sleepy look and scrawny backswing, weighing 70 pounds if you counted the Shetland wool pullover clinging to his bony frame, came in with a 5.

Willie Park, of Musselburgh, winner of the first Open Championship, lends his commanding presence to a stairway in the Royal and Ancient Golf Club of St. Andrews. Park beat Old Tom Morris by two strokes in the inaugural event, contested by eight professionals at the Prestwick Club in 1860.

If the passion that golfers from all walks of life, of all ages, and of virtually every nationality can be captured in images, it is in those visual reminders of the romance and heritage of this happy, yet complicated, pursuit. At least, that has been our objective in assembling *A Passion for Golf*. The collective consciousness of golf is not found in the aerial views of the great courses, or the swing sequences of the great golfers, or the impressive statistics of the golf record book. Rather, it is found in the interstices of club life, public and private, famous and unknown, where art, craft, collections, local customs, and quotidian scenes forge golf's unique, imperishable identity.

The stolid sandstone clubhouse of the R & A, built in 1854, functions both as a private club of 1,800 members, including an overseas membership of 750, and as governing authority for the game of golf in all countries of the world except the United States, Canada, and Mexico.

Anyway, the pictures of the R & A, now that I have bathed in their glow, have thawed my perception of our harsh winter up here in the Berkshires. Now I see that the snow is positively in retreat over our mowing. Puddles exist in nature again. Crocuses appear, along with the first crop of mud.

And so I've begun sleeping without my socks on, and taking creaky practice swings in the barn, and stroking putts against the grain on the Oriental rug.

Given all that, I am not surprised to pick up the phone and hear the urgent voice of Baxter.

"I think we could probably get in nine holes tomorrow," he says in his husky voice.

"The course is closed," I reply tactfully. Mind you, Baxter and I have not spoken in months. But at once we are immersed in the arcane parlance of the golfing brotherhood.

A rack, originally built for top hats, accommodates more casual attire in high style, in a corridor of the world's most celebrated golf club.

"The club parking lot has not been plowed since the Christmas pro shop sale," I point out. "The temporary greens are buried under ice and snow." Throwing in some italics for special effect, I repeat to my golfing buddy, "The course is *closed!*"

"I've checked," says Baxter. "Ten, eleven, and twelve, up on the hill, are playable. That goddamn north wind's kept most of the snow off, you see, and the snowmobilers have actually turned the greens into a decent putting surface. So we could play them three times—once, of course, backwards—to make our nine."

"That's different. What time shall we meet?"

The golfer's compulsive nature, never more so than at the brink of spring, is superficially explored in the heroic couplets of Thomas Mathison, from a poem that is the oldest known literary

The beloved Old Tom Morris, four times Open champion, served as the keeper of the green in St. Andrews for nearly 40 years.

tribute to the game. Mathison was a clergyman in Edinburgh, Scotland, when he wrote "The Goff." His 18th-century version of golf as expressed in the title makes the game sound like a mythical beast, or a weather pattern, or some obscure, incurable malady, and all of those meanings hold some water, come to think of it.

Men of the cloth still sermonize about the game, for golf lends itself to parable and platitude in a way that few sporting endeavors do. There is the Old Testament, the New Testament, and the Scorecard Testament. The game is a convenient metaphor. Golf can be a journey, a quest, a test; on an off day, it can be a trip before the Stations of the Cross, or a battle with (a) the Ball, (b) the Golf Course, (c) the Opponent, or (d) the Self. Or it is a tragedy in two acts: Front 9 and Back 9.

Nongolfers hold the game in such contempt because its influence is so pervasive on friends who have been lost to the pursuit. Calling it "the game of a lifetime," they reason, is a euphemism for the life sentence without parole.

Even in boom years golf has many disapprovers. The Greenpeacenik is appalled by the vast acreage devoted to such an idle passion. The Jock prefers a more vigorous sport like skiing or tennis; the Couch Potato favors the vicarious pleasure of watching team sports like baseball, football, and basketball. The Reformer deplores the exclusionary nature, by design or happenstance, of such an expensive and time-consuming activity. The Hedonist recoils from golf's delayed gratification. It takes 99 strokes or less to complete an 18-hole test with a score of less than 100, and most golfers lack the skills and concentration to string together that many "good shots" to do it. But, then, most golfers are in deep denial about their inability to break 100, fair and square. As for scaling the palisades of par, only an elite few manage it consistently, most of them—the godlike pros—being paid handsomely for their troubles.

Hitting a silly little ball around" is today's derogatory version of "invading the skies by playing the jointed club." It is often voiced by someone who has never played the game, or who has had a traumatic early encounter with it. "Golf is a good walk spoiled," noted Mark Twain, the only misspoken thought in the great man's canon.

But calumnies and slander about golf routinely issue from its most devoted followers, too. When Baxter called the other day, it brought to mind the

The Big Room of the R & A clubhouse (OPPOSITE), its original lockers now mainly in disuse, contains portraits of Queen Elizabeth, HRH the Duke of Windsor (who was captain of the club in 1922), and other bluebloods. The room overlooks the first tee of the Old Course (BELOW), where more than 40,000 rounds are played every year, most of them by tourists.

A View of the Golf Course, above the fireplace in the Card Room of the R & A, was painted by W. M. Fraser in 1861.

last round we had played together late last fall.

You see, I had come to the 14th hole needing a par or bogey to stay in the match. The 14th at Hickory Ridge is a short dogleg par-4, but it does require a manful carry from the tee of about 185 yards to clear a stream.

No problem. I selected my 3-wood, caressed the persimmon thing of beauty (and expense), and let 'er fly. The ball flew dangerously near a tree gowned in autumn foliage, nicked a limb, and then dropped like a wounded quail where the stream ran.

Not to worry. There was a good chance the ball had stayed on the far bank, if only I could find it among the leaves. Meanwhile, Baxter, sensing his chance to close me out, laid up in front of the stream with a 6-iron, as craven and wimpish a shot as Hickory Ridge had seen in a long time. I was sorely nettled.

After watching Baxter play his second shot as cautiously as the first, clearing the gulch but falling well

short of the bunker guarding the front of the green, I crossed the rustic footbridge, descended the bank, and, *mirabile dictu,* came upon my ball sitting up pretty as a picture.

The steep bank obviated the possibility of going for the green, but a well-struck wedge (smooth backswing!) would put me astride Baxter's ball and keep me in the hole. Whereupon I took out my p.w. and executed perfectly, I don't mind saying, except for one thing.

With the severe sidehill stance, I had inadvertently opened the face of my club so that when it made contact with the ball, it was actually pointing slightly behind me, back toward the tee.

And that is where the ball headed. It shot like a bolt crisply backwards and high, striking the same branch I had nicked on the tee shot, and plummeted into the swirling waters below. The water magnified my Titleist 3, and for a moment it glowed like the stricken face of Desdemona.

When I hit the ball, I had known my mechanics and timing were sound, and for an iota of time I

lived in smug anticipation of a fine result. I had not even lost my balance—and, generally speaking, I fall down after hitting from an uneven lie.

In any case, the rude awakening caused me to stare in disbelief at Baxter. To give him his due, Baxter appeared to be suppressing

Daily, lunch unfolds in decorous fashion in the all-male refuge (LEFT). The statue of Lady Heathcoat-Amory (OPPOSITE), who as Joyce Wethered dominated British women's golf in the 1920s, was given to the club in 1974. Her brother Roger, himself a leading amateur, was captain of the R & A in 1946.

an urge to laugh out loud at the surprise trick shot he had just witnessed. Baxter, of course, would go on to win the hole by reaching the green in 3, then 3-putting for a workmanlike 6.

It had been years since I had last thrown a club. The wedge flew down the left side of the fairway end-over-end and was last seen entering a stand

The R & A's finest painting, *Ice on the Scheldt*, by a 17th-century Dutch master, depicts kolf being played on a frozen canal in Holland. This was a different game from golf. The "apprentice clubs" were made by Willie Auchterlonie in about 1890, and Laurie Auchterlonie in 1922. Before the age of the fax machine, queries in elegant hands about the Rules of Golf (BELOW) arrived at the club from around the world.

of some cattails with a satisfying whoosh.

Golf is indeed an unpredictable game, full of happy-go-lucky bounces, rude surprises, and subtle tests of personality, character, and I.Q. Take golf too seriously and you will not enjoy a minute of it. Relax unduly during play, and you will play a different tune and pay a higher price.

In fact, the game's appeal lies in large part in its vexing complexity, but self-induced mistakes, such as my dismal performance outlined above, are not the only blots on the card.

For example, I was playing Portmarnock, one of the glories of Irish golf. It was a blustery day in

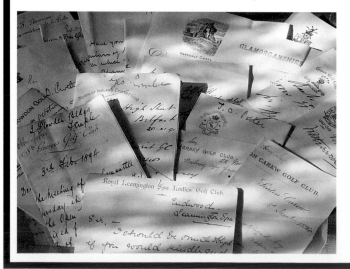

October, when sensible folk had their feet up by a peat fire, or were throwing darts in the neighborhood pub. So desolate was the setting it felt as if my caddie, a gent of indeterminate age by the name of Lonergan, and I were the last people left on earth.

Portmarnock is a championship links, treeless as the moon, pounded by the Irish Sea, drenched in the blood of the best golfers in all of Europe, and damned hard to play on a calm day from the ladies' tees (which exist only as a reluctant afterthought at Portmarnock). In its windblown and rain-spattered beauty on this day, Portmarnock was impossible, at least for a golfer of my limited skills. Nonetheless, I was happy as a clam to be slogging through its dramatic landscapes, and playing like a clam, too.

Lonergan, in his ill-fitting dark suit, was taciturn to a fault, and none of my bad shots had an effect on him one way or another. It may have been the tranquilizing effects of the pipe on which he sucked from time to time, clenched in his teeth with the bowl upside down.

When we caught up with the only other players on the course that day—a foursome of pink-faced clerics, still with their Roman collars on—it was proper for the group to invite me, playing alone, to play through. There was no way around it. So I teed

The balcony from the office of the Secretary of the R & A offers a sweeping view of the Firth of Tay and the links land where golf found a congenial setting as early as 1457 (the year King James II of Scotland banned the game because it interfered with archery practice among his subjects). Directly below the balcony is the first tee and starter's box for the Old Course.

up my ball and with an apologetic nod to the company—the Irish think practice swings are a nuisance and a waste of time—I took a practice swing.

I mention this because the practice swing surely gave Lonergan ample opportunity to notice my stance and the line of play I had in mind for my drive. Yet no corrective peep came from the man.

And so I teed off a good 60 degrees starboard of where I was supposed to go. I had driven the ball toward a green in the distance, but it was the wrong green. Not yet realizing this, I retrieved my tee and straightened to my full height. For at this juncture, I was unmindful of all but the fact that I had just produced my very best drive of the week. The priests, by contrast, were open-mouthed with amazement at my misdeed, as if I had executed a

Among the R & A's prized medals and trophies are the Silver Club, with silver and gold balls appended, competed for, along with the captaincy, from 1754 to 1824; the Calcutta Cup, made in India from melted-down rupees in 1882; the Queen Victoria Jubilee Vase, dating from 1887; and the Silver Beaver, presented by R & A members in Canada in 1966 to mark the Canadian Centenary.

SPRING
BEGINNINGS

THE NEW GOLF YEAR BEGINS ON A
HIGH NOTE, WITH THE GRASS
GREEN, THE AIR FRESH, AND THE
SLATE CLEAN. THE GOLFER STEPS
ON THE FIRST TEE WITH RENEWED
HOPE AND PERHAPS MISPLACED
CONFIDENCE. THE PERPETUAL
NEWNESS OF THE GAME IS NEVER
MORE EVIDENT THAN NOW.

"Caddies must at all times keep off the club porches."
—FROM "GUIDELINES FOR PROSPECTIVE CADDIES," NEW HAVEN COUNTRY CLUB, CIRCA 1948

After its long and quirky gestation in the links lands of St. Andrews, the Lothians and eastern shore, and Aberdeen in Scotland, golf spread to the Continent and to North America. In visiting some of the earliest sites of the old game in new places, we encountered such impressive edifices as Newport, host to America's first national amateur and open championships in 1895, and St. Cloud, five minutes from the Arc de Triomphe in Paris, 11 times host to the French Open, and as stylish now as it was when an American lawyer founded it in 1911.

Newport, by the way, is one of the five founding clubs of the U.S. Golf Association, handmaiden to the Rules of Golf in the United States, sponsor of the national championships that began at Newport, and spiritual cohort of the Royal and Ancient (R & A) in Scotland. Together, the USGA and the R & A constitute a kind of Vatican for the golfing faithful, complete with sacred relics and men in funny clothes.

By contrast, there are historic golf clubs that time has all but forgotten, such as Morfontaine, cloaked in the verdant secrecy of a forest north of Paris; or Niagara-on-the-Lake in Canada; or Otsego in Cooperstown, New York; or Foxburg in eastern Pennsylvania, where oil, and oil wealth, once flowed like water. When we finally located these places, it was

with a peculiar appreciation for both the past and the future of golf that we cast our gaze.

For, just as the game humbly reinvents itself on newly turned soils, a passion for the game usually starts in the pristine environment of youth and ignorance. In fact, the first impression golf makes, particularly on the young, can mold one's life, or scar it.

This is a universal truth; only the details that color each beginning are different. Whether you picked up the game in Dornoch or Dorchester or Dieppe or Dallas, the formative influences and sensory ambience of the game's original setting remain with you.

If, copying a favorite baseball player, you learned to operate a golf club with a flat swing and 10-fingered grip, chances are you still produce prodigious left-to-right tee shots into the Great Smokies. If some early benefactor told you to hook all your putts, à la Bobby Locke, chances are you are still in thrall to that iffy technique—iffy for everyone except Locke.

Because golf is played more or less in nature, with an infinite variety of regional and climatic differences, most of us have made seemingly bizarre subconscious horticultural associations with the game. Today, for instance, the smell of freshly mown grass in early spring, when the grass is bursting with nutrients and looks sweet enough to eat, is a sensation that still transports me, albeit briefly, to when I first set forth on a golf course, a half-pint with a crewcut, five unmatched clubs, and large, bewildered eyes.

Only my spring allergies keep me from succumbing to nostalgia.

In the town where I grew up, there could not have been two more contrasting golf facilities than the Meadowbrook Golf Club and the New Haven Country Club. They were the *Upstairs, Downstairs* of the golfing world, and I caddied at both of them.

It took me years to shake off the mistaken ideas that I formulated during the summers when I was 10, 11, and 12—namely, that the only good golfers were WASPs, and that the only good tippers were working-class men.

eadowbrook was a shoestring operation run by a local farming family trying to come up in the world from sweet corn and McIntosh apples. The words that make clubmen grind their teeth— OPEN TO THE PUBLIC—were posted in tilting individual block letters on the roof of the rickety old colonial used as the clubhouse, with Christmas lights permanently entwined among the letters.

At Meadowbrook, the fairways turned into brown cement every summer, and the water hazards began to smell so bad my caddie friends and I would have to forgo our evening dives in search of lost golf balls. But it wasn't a bad layout. There were some challenging one-shotters, and the back 9, cut through a piney woods, had a lot of narrow landing areas. One hole, I think it was the 7th, played up a hill so steep it couldn't be mowed, so the approach to the green was invariably played out of knee-high milkweed and thistle.

Most of the guys who played at Meadowbrook did things for a living I could understand. They cut hair or sold shoes or delivered mail. They were stone masons, cops, pizza parlor operators, car mechanics.

Some of them had decent golf games, but most just muscled the ball around the course, slicing their tee shots, chili-dipping their pitches, and hoping for the best.

New Haven, I suppose, was a typical pillars-of-society club, founded in 1895 by Theodore S. Woolsey, a Yale law professor, and Justus S. Hotchkiss, a local business mogul.  Its well-groomed course was set between fetching Lake Whitney on one side and the many-mansioned Old Hartford Turnpike on the other. The likes of Harry Vardon and William Howard Taft had played here. Newspaper publisher John Day Jackson (his *New Haven Register* was the paper my parents read with Democratic hostility every day) was a member. A genuine Scotsman, Bobby Andrew, had been the pro for years; some of his pronouncements had entered the club's collective memory, such as: "Keep your bustle out of your drive and put it in your putt."

I remember wondering exactly what Bobby meant when I first read about his bustles on one of my unauthorized forays onto "the club porches." I still wonder.

New Haven CC golfers dressed up in corduroy and tweed to play golf and a lot of them had panatelas jutting from between their teeth. Between shots, they spoke of "whole life" and "income tax" and "debentures" and "irresponsible, reprehensible Roosevelt." Their bags were heavy. They played with new balls, not range balls, and they were adamant about rules and etiquette. Except for the doctors, who attacked the course on Wednesdays with their largely haphazard and temperamental games, the male golfers at New Haven were at least consistent, and there was a fair number of low-handicappers among them. You didn't have to spend a lot of time searching out balls in the woods at New Haven, as you did at Meadowbrook.

I was not the dutiful, scholarship-winning breed of caddie, I'm sorry to say. There was so much more money to be made playing cards with other no-account kids. At New Haven, I was paid $1.25 a bag, and if I carried double, plus tip, I might go home with $3. But I could make $20 or $25 playing Yiddish poker, blackjack, or 7-card stud, low hole-card wild.

Needless to say, I gave up gaming pursuits when I realized they were a question mark on my character, but at the time I enjoyed raking in pot after pot. I was so lucky at cards that I rarely had a losing day. The other caddies started calling me, not without a modicum of spite and envy, "Full Boat." The winnings did help me support my two older brothers, who were having girlfriend and cash-flow problems at the time. I charged them a mere 10 cents on the dollar for gas money and prom expenses.

Card-playing was frowned on by the caddie master at New Haven, so we organized our games out of sight, underneath a lyrical suspension bridge that spanned a neck of the lake, connecting the club grounds with the section of town where the Whitney Movie Theater was located—makeout headquarters for teenagers and a welcome sanctuary for caddies on a rainy summer day.

Come to think of it, my pals Bruce Guthrie and Bobby Messier also played a lot of cards between loops at the club, and yet they developed into far better golfers than I. They easily made the high school golf team a couple of years later, which became their passport out of algebra class on interminable Friday afternoons. Guthrie and Messier were built alike, lanky and mean as the proverbial 1-iron, and they had the courageously long, flowing backswings I learned to emulate only after years of assertiveness training.

All golfers have early swing models like Guthrie and Messier wired into their memory trace. They are the players we expected to show up on television one day, winning the odd Masters or Open, such was their grace and power off the tee, such was their aplomb in the rough, such was their mastery of the short game, when we were young and impressionable.

After college, golf briefly lost its appeal—so much for higher education. It was not that I had given up on the game, but that the game had given up on me. True, the ancient MacGregors my cousin had bequeathed me were no longer the stuff of par performance, what with their grips and hosels perpetually unwinding, and the inserts on the wood faces rattling like old teeth whenever I took the club back. But on my cub reporter's salary at the *Hartford Courant* I could hardly afford to replace them.

And so, if it were sunny on Mondays and Tuesdays, my days off, I would throw the clubs on my shoulder and take the bus—two buses, actually—to Goodwin Park and play the public course there, almost always with postmen, as it happened. They were older guys who liked to advise me to apply pressure to the club with my pinkies for extra distance on my drives, and to drink clam juice for virility. One always paid off his debts in stamps purloined from his postmaster.

After this dispiriting interval, I obtained a new lease on golfing life in a way I could never have predicted. Faced with being drafted for two years, I decided to enlist in the Army for three, with the goal of seeing Europe at government expense. I was assigned to a supply garrison in eastern France, and there discovered golf course architecture as it is conceived by the Army Corps of Engineers.

Verdun-sur-Meuse Golf Club was a 9-holer laid out, for the exclusive use of the U.S. military, on condemned farmland amid the battlefields where over a million French and German infantrymen fell during nine months in 1916. There were still so many unexploded *obus* buried in the countryside from that nightmare in trench warfare that, a half-century later, golfers were still being advised to take very shallow divots.

In addition to the odd artillery shell going off, there were other hazards—misaligned teeing grounds, crisscrossing fairways, bunkers made of chunky limestone, standing water everywhere after a rain, and greens sprouting with wild onions. They all contributed to the tactical challenge and spirit of adventure at Verdun-sur-Meuse GC. But for two and a half years, flaws and all, it was my "home club," my very first experience with the privileges of membership, with neither the large expense nor many of the social responsibilities. Here I entertained the French friends I had cultivated in my job as an extremely low low-level intelligence agent. Although the French have since seen the light, most of the natives of Lorraine at that time sniffed at golf as a suspicious Anglo-Saxon import.

The French tour of duty completed my formation as a golfer. Most travelers bone up on wine and cheese when they go to France. I learned about ball compression, shaft flex, club selection, stepping off yardages, reading greens, and all the other basic components of playing the game—all the things Guthrie and Messier had known but failed to tell me, possibly because they thought I wasn't interested or worthy. I figured out the courtesies to show other golfers in my foursome, even if they were officers. I bought my first pair of spikes. I mastered the lateral water hazard rule. I even had my own locker, combination 11-42-07-15 (my Army serial number).

My beginnings as a golfer were finally over, a stage that lasted longer for me than for most golfers, but probably not so different from the common experience of apprenticeship to the game. Henceforth I would always feel comfortable in any golf setting, whether a place as fine and private as Royal Aberdeen, or a bustling golf center like Pinehurst, or a remote fastness in the New England hills like Ashfield Community Golf Club. They are all the same, really—properties defined, maintained, and bound together by an abiding passion and fascination for an old game.

But as timeworn and traditional as golf may be, its perpetual newness strikes me hard each spring, when the smell of first-mown green grass is in the air.

When the shingle and wood clubhouse at Newport was completed in 1895, it immediately became a mecca for society, and the *New York Times* proclaimed, "It stood supreme for magnificence among golf clubs, not only in America, but in the world." Its architect, Ecole-des-Beaux-Arts-trained Whitney Warren, went on to design Grand Central Terminal, the Broadmoor in Colorado, and other hotels and railway buildings.

roaring personal success for Vardon and an absolute revelation to American golfers," writes golf historian Robert Sommers.

Golf had arrived in America through transplanted Scotsmen, like John Reid and Robert Lockhart, who founded St. Andrews Golf Club in Yonkers, New York, in 1888, or through well-to-do American sports like Charles B. Macdonald, William K. Vanderbilt, and Theodore Havemeyer, who brought the game home with them from their travels. Macdonald embraced the game while a student at St. Andrews University in Scotland, and became a fine amateur player and golf architect. He designed one of America's first 18-hole courses for Chicago Golf Club in 1895. Vanderbilt organized Shinnecock Hills on Long Island after watching Scottish professional Willie Dunn give an exhibition in Biarritz, France. "Gentlemen, this beats rifle shooting for distance and accuracy," he told his associates. "It is a game I think would go in our country." Sugar magnate Theodore Havemeyer discovered the game while vacationing at the venerable golf resort of Pau, France, "the St. Andrews of the Continent," in 1899. Upon his return he set about to organize the Newport Country Club and the first unofficial national golf championships in 1894. Later Havemeyer would also serve as the first

The USGA, headquartered in Far Hills, New Jersey (ABOVE), was organized in 1894, at a dinner at the Calumet Club in New York City, by representatives of five clubs: Newport; St. Andrews in Yonkers; Shinnecock Hills on Long Island; the Country Club in Brookline, Massachusetts; and the Chicago Golf Club.

In Golf House, the USGA's estimable museum in Far Hills, New Jersey, a 1919 painting by Allan Stewart, *The First International Foursome*, depicts a match between England and Scotland on Leith Links in 1682 (OPPOSITE). The Women's Amateur trophy on the mantel (RIGHT), enamel on silver with topaz insets, was first won by Miss Beatrix Hoyt, playing out of Shinnecock Hills Golf Club in 1896.

president of the United States Golf Association.

From a handful of clubs in the formative 1880s, golf spread to more than a thousand locations by the time Vardon toured America. In subsequent years, the growth accelerated as golf became more familiar to the general public, and players like Walter Travis, Walter Hagen, and Gene Sarazen began to make

their mark in the major tournaments. The last vestiges of skepticism about the Scottish game among Americans were wiped out when one of their own, Francis Ouimet, an unknown amateur, beat Harry Vardon and Ted Ray in a historic playoff at the Country Club in Brookline for the 1913 U.S. Open championship.

The Mexican Amateur Championship Trophy (ABOVE), crafted by Michoacan silversmith Jacinto Vigueras and first awarded in 1926, is one of many objects at Golf House that speak to the universality of the game, in this case in symbols derived from both Aztec and Toltec cultures, including the figure of the water goddess at the top, club in hand.

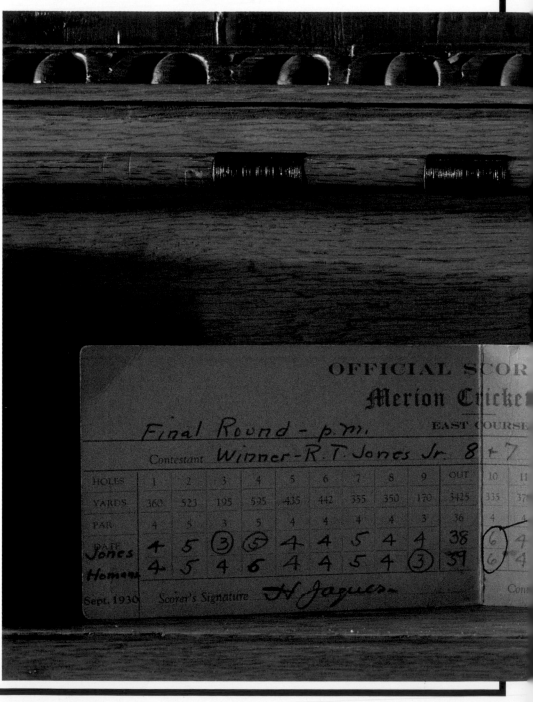

If Ouimet came as John the Baptist to proclaim America's profound and lasting affinity for golf, Bobby Jones would prove to be its Messiah. At age 12, he won his club championship at East Lake Country Club in Atlanta, Georgia. At age 13, he was proclaimed a "golf marvel" in the nation's press when he went around East Lake in 5-under-par 68,

In addition to its extensive book collection (LEFT), Golf House offers a glimpse of the career of America's most enduring golf champion, in the Bobby Jones Room (BELOW). The scorecard that records the conclusion of Jones's Grand Slam in 1930 sits happily atop a mantel, along with the Spalding Dot used to sink the final putt.

to tie the course record held by the club's professional, Stewart Maiden, a native of Carnoustie, Scotland. Competing as a chubby 14-year-old in the 1916 U.S. Amateur, Jones led the field in the first day's qualifying, a feat that prompted predictions of greatness. But several years of frustration and disappointment in tournament golf lay ahead for Jones, until he won his first major title, the 1923 U.S. Open title at Inwood Country Club on Long Island.

As more championships came his way, Jones achieved a unique celebrity. Britain's Alistair Cooke best identified the gifted Southerner's impact in *America*, many years after Jones managed the stupendous feat of winning the four major golf championships of his era in the same year. In Jones, wrote Cooke, "the 1920s was saluting an old ideal in the moment of its passing . . . something America hungered for and found, the best performer in the world who was also a hero human being, the gentle, chivalrous, wholly self-sufficient male, Jefferson's lost paragon: the wise innocent."

In the dining room at East Lake (BELOW), a reminder of the Bobby Jones legacy exists as a typical group foursome photo, annotated "last 18 holes played" by Jones, over which, in 1948, he shot a 72 at the home course.

East Lake Country Club (ABOVE, LEFT, AND OPPOSITE) in Atlanta, Georgia, where Bobby Jones first learned to play golf, holds many memories of the man who brought skill, intelligence, character, and humor to the game.

The oldest surviving golf course in North America, Niagara-on-the-Lake (LEFT), is a short 9-holer bounded by Lake Ontario, Fort Mississauga, and the stately homes of one of Canada's earliest summer resorts.

EARLY GOLF OUTPOSTS
Pioneering Clubs of the New World

The first golf clubs organized in North America, and still in existence today, were in Canada—Royal Montreal, in 1873, and Royal Quebec, in 1875. The latter club is now almost exclusively French-speaking, but it was a Scotsman, James Hunter, the son-in-law of Old Tom Morris, who was the catalyst for its formation when he visited Quebec City in that year on business for the Bank of British North America. Like golfing businessmen ever since, Hunter traveled with his clubs, and he inspired "a smouldering enthusiasm" for golf when the fine amateur gave a demonstration of how the game was supposed to be played.

Both venerable Canadian clubs moved from their original sites years ago. But Niagara-on-the-

Niagara-on-the-Lake (BELOW), a flat, tree-lined course, opened for play in 1878 and "bid fair to become the St. Andrews of Canada," according to an early club captain, when golf surged in popularity in the 1890s. Many of its trophies (RIGHT) date from the early part of this century, including the Hunter Cup, inscribed to the Queens Royal GC in 1907, and the Militia Cup, presented to the club by officers in training at Camp Niagara in 1924.

Niagara's Ladies Lounge (OPPOSITE) bespeaks the competitive side of club life. The Niagara International, staged here in 1895, was the first golf tournament of its kind in North America, won by Charles B. Macdonald a month before his U.S. Amateur victory at Newport. "The club may have been overtaken by time and events, its grand days long forgotten," writes the Canadian golf historian James A. Barclay of Niagara-on-the-Lake, "but it remains not only a visible and symbolic link between Canada and the United States, but a memorial to the pioneer golfers of both nations."

Lake Golf Club in Ontario, seven miles from Niagara Falls, New York, still plays over a 9-hole course first used in 1880 or 1881, according to James A. Barclay, author of the monumental history *Golf in Canada,* which makes this the oldest surviving golf course in North America.

Once one of the premier golf clubs of Canada, Niagara-on-the-Lake is now largely forgotten except by its loyal members and by golfing visitors to the town's annual George Bernard Shaw Festival, who make the happy discovery of the short layout, with its expansive views of the Toronto skyline, across Lake Ontario, 35 miles away, and of pugnacious Fort Niagara on the American side.

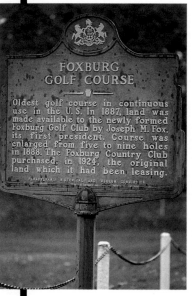

Charles B. Macdonald, that ubiquitous presence in early American golf, brought a team of men and women golfers from Chicago and New York to compete in the first Niagara International Golf Tournament in 1895. Playing the gutta-percha ball, he won that year's long-drive contest—distance has always been an obsession in golf—with a blow of 179 yards. The Niagara International became an annual event on the club's calendar, touted as the first tournament in the New World open to amateur golfers of all nations, and with events for both sexes. It attracted a lively field for a week of social and competitive golf until World War I brought the tournament, and the easeful way of life of Niagara's privileged classes of the Edwardian era, to an abrupt end.

Foxburg Country Club, located high above the Allegheny River in Clarion County of western Pennsylvania, claims to be the oldest golf course in continuous use in the United States, and so provides an intriguing historical counterpart to Niagara. The course lies on land once owned by Joseph M. Fox. Writing in *Golf Digest,* Ross Goodner reported that

Foxburg Country Club in western Pennsylvania (RIGHT), dating from the 1820s, was originally the residence of Joseph M. Fox, heir to an oil fortune who introduced golf to Foxburg after seeing the game and meeting Old Tom Morris in St. Andrews in 1884. The oldest entry in the players' log (OPPOSITE) notes that Mr. and Mrs. H. J. Thomson of Pittsburgh paid $1.50 each in green fees on August 1, 1929.

Fox had played cricket at Haverford College and later at Merion Cricket Club. It was while playing amateur cricket matches for Merion in Britain in 1884 that Fox discovered golf.

Returning to Foxburg with clubs (left-handed) and balls acquired in Scotland, Fox laid out a 5-hole course on his family's estate in 1887, adding four more holes the next year. The greens were made of sand, with 1-quart tomato cans for the cups. Greenskeepers erased footprints on the sand greens with a long pole with a burlap bag nailed to the end. After the player had putted out, club records show that a man named John Dunkle was hired at a salary of $15 a year to keep the fairways groomed with his scythe.

The discovery of oil in the Foxburg area following the Civil War had produced a large number of wealthy families. It is surmised that one reason golf caught on so quickly

Past and present permeate Foxburg's modest locker room (ABOVE), where records of earlier club championships (OPPOSITE) preserve notable rounds even as scores fade from the page and from memory.

when Fox brought it back with him from Scotland was that so many young men in the area had the leisure and inclination to take a stab at a "royal and ancient" game.

An unpretentious exhibit area inside the log clubhouse pays tribute to Foxburg's early history with displays of wood clubs from the gutta-percha

A poster of Sam Snead (ABOVE), distributed by Wilson Sporting Goods when he and Ben Hogan dominated professional golf in the 1940s and 1950s, hangs in the Foxburg clubhouse, still a model of swing tempo and effortless power for today's club members (RIGHT).

era, including clubs made by Young Tom Morris, of St. Andrews, Scotland, and the legendary Douglas J. McEwan, of Bruntsfield and Musselburgh. Incongruously, there is also a collection of the funny hats, giant tees, and many-jointed clubs of Joe Kirkwood, the immensely talented trick-shot artist of the 1940s and 1950s. But, then, golf is both a solemn and a comic affair wherever it is played or remembered.

Cooperstown, New York, is better known as the birthplace of James Fenimore Cooper and the home of the Baseball Hall of Fame, but here, too, is a rustic old club rich in golfing heritage. Otsego Golf Club began as a 12-hole layout in 1894, adjoining the limpid waters of Otsego Lake, dubbed "Glimmerglass" by Cooper, where lake steamers named after characters from his novels, including

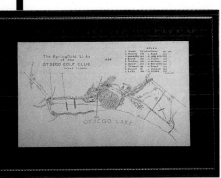

Natty Bumppo and Mohican, formerly carried summer travelers.

Like many vintage watering places, Otsego has been something of a family business for generations. Arthur Clarke, the current president, is a descendent of two of the founders, G. Hyde Clarke and Leslie Pell-Clarke.

An 1888 farmhouse (ABOVE), moved from the shore of Otsego Lake, serves as the clubhouse of the Otsego Golf Club of Springfield and Cooperstown, as it was called when founded in 1894.

His uncle, John B. Ryerson, virtually ran the club singlehanded from 1940 to 1967, when he resigned to pave the way for the club's incorporation.

Jack Ryerson was a golfing zealot whose exploits were celebrated in Ripley's "Believe It or Not." A strip appearing in 1954 reported he had played 1,015 different golf courses in 36 years.

Most of the 19 founding members of Otsego are memorialized on a wall in the clubhouse (OPPOSITE), including Leslie Pell-Clarke, below lamp, who owned the land. Another founder, A. B. Cox, drew the schematic (ABOVE LEFT) that shows the original 12 holes. A tribute to lifelong member John B. Ryerson (RIGHT) includes records of holes-in-one at Pine Valley and Pebble Beach.

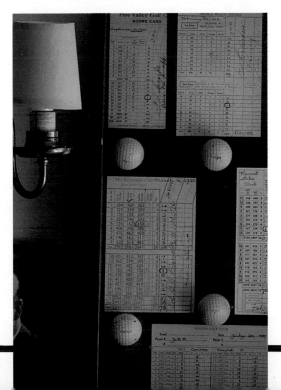

Golf de St.-Cloud, founded by an American lawyer, Henry Cachard, in 1911, was built on the land of the Castle of Buzenval, outside Paris, once owned by Napoleon's wife, Josephine. The first of its two courses was laid out by British architect Henry S. Colt in 1913. The clubhouse, built in 1923, was designed by the French architect, Louis Sue.

APRIL IN PARIS
Golf Spreads to the Continent

Golf was first played in France by Scottish troops in the army of Arthur Wellesley, the Duke of Wellington, who were garrisoned near Pau, in the south of France, following the defeat of Napoleon at Waterloo. Several officers later returned to Pau to build a golf course in 1856, Europe's first, which to this day is known as "the St. Andrews of the Continent," even though a contemporary chronicler of French golf, Alain R. Bucquet, refers to the historic emplacement as "more like English golf on French territory" than a genuine Gallic commitment to the game. This, Bucquet argues with some justice, did not begin until Pierre Deschamps, known as "the father of golf in France," returned from playing several courses in the United States, filled with such enthusiasm that he built La Boulie, in 1901, on a tract of hilly farmland in Versailles, near Paris.

Other sports-minded Parisians

At Golf de St.-Cloud, the international language of golf surfaces in novelty tournaments (ABOVE) that call for putts to be made *main gauche seule*—holding the putter with the left hand only—or *tranche du SW*—with the flange end of the sand wedge. But no matter what the language, the 19th hole (OPPOSITE) is always easy to identify.

One of France's most prestigious golf clubs, Golf de St.-Cloud (RIGHT) is located less than five miles from Place de l'Étoile in Paris, on a ridge where the French and Prussians fought the Battle of Buzenval in 1871. The Green Course (ABOVE RIGHT) is a hilly, parkland layout, 6,540 yards long, with tree-lined fairways.

Chantilly Golf Club, north of Paris, boasts a handsome clubhouse (ABOVE) and a championship golf course, designed in 1906 by the British architect Tom Simpson, where important niceties of golf (BELOW), such as repairing pitch marks and replacing divots, are de rigueur. A table is set up on the first tee (RIGHT) for sending off contestants in a timely fashion.

REPAREZ vos PITCHS
REMETTEZ vos DIVOTS

Inside the clubhouse (OPPOSITE), tournament mementos collect under an honor roll of members who lost their lives on the battlefield. Winners of the French Open when it was played at Chantilly include Arnaud Massy, Henry Cotton, Roberto de Vicenzo, Peter Oosterhuis, and Nick Faldo.

formed clubs at Chantilly, St.-Cloud, Morfontaine, and St.-Germain. Still going strong, these clubs provide the most revealing glimpse into the timeless character and style of the European golf tradition, while St.-Nom-la-Breteche shows how even a relatively new club, founded in 1959, enjoys an air of antiquity thanks to its extraordinary site.

Other early milestones in the development of French golf occurred in 1911, with the publication of the first golf book in French, *Le Golf*, by France's most accomplished professional golfer, Arnaud Massy; in 1912, with the formation of what would become the Federation Française de Golf (FFG); and in 1914, with the publication of the first golf periodical, *Tennis et Golf*, which later became the official organ of the FFG. Today there are more than 450 golf courses registered with the FFG, twice the number of a decade

ASSOCIATION SPORTIVE
DU GOLF DE CHANTILLY

ago, and second in number among European nations only to Great Britain. (Germany and Sweden are also rapidly moving into the ranks of golf fanatics.)

The French golfing population has quadrupled, from 50,000 to 200,000, in the same time period. With so many novices in the game today, it is not surprising that the rational French have come up with some impressive methods for schooling their golfing naifs. Three-hole practice layouts have been built adjoining full-length courses for the benefit of the beginner. Practice facilities have been designed to allow the student golfer to work on all aspects of the game without prematurely coming to grief on the golf course. All this works to the benefit of the more accomplished golfer, too—there are fewer inconveniences to cope with and wait upon during one's round.

The extraordinary élan with which the French channel their passion for golf shows up in different ways. The

Caricatures made by a member at Chantilly in the 1940s (LEFT) capture the Gallic profiles of fellow members "Dupont" and "Carnot," who undoubtedly owed some of their sartorial elegance to regularly spiffing up in the club's *vestiare,* or locker room (RIGHT).

Parisian clubs project an image of restraint, stylish fashions, and unpretentious refinement. The Basque country around Biarritz has clubs with a rustic, convivial atmosphere, along with many of France's best teaching professionals. At one of the many *villages-golf* created by Club Med, golf is a diversion for some, a serious learning experience for others. It is a serious sensory experience if you play the Cognac Golf Club, near Bordeaux, in October: it's grape-pressing season, on fairways that wind through the vineyards of Martell, in an atmosphere that is literally intoxicating. (Apropos, a good wine celler is as important to a French golf club as a well-stocked pro shop.)

Morfontaine began as a 9-hole course in 1913, then, in 1927, it commissioned the English architect Tom Simpson, who had designed the neighboring Chantilly, to add an 18-hole layout. Hitting the official opening drive was Simone Thion de la Chaumes, who later

Trees hovering on the ideal line of flight exact their toll on the par-3 13th hole at Morfontaine (BELOW). The club's tee markers (INSET, LEFT) are as distinctive as the trophy, a wood-shafted gold putter, on the fireplace mantel in the club's reading room (LEFT). The first foursome to tee off on the original 9-hole course at Morfontaine in 1913 was James Braid, Arnaud Massy, Jean Grassiat, and the Duke de Gramont.

Although less than 40 years old, the 36-hole complex of St.-Nom-la-Breteche draws on its 16th-century buildings for considerable ambience, as in its inviting dining room (ABOVE).

An antique architectural frame (OPPOSITE) has been adapted to show off in resplendent style a roster of club champions. In the club entry (RIGHT), a blackboard keeps members up to date on tournament activity. Pull carts (ABOVE) are the golf-bag carriers of choice at St.-Nom, as at most French clubs.

married tennis great René LaCoste, "The Crocodile." Their daughter, Catherine LaCoste, the 1967 U.S. Women's Open champion, established the course record at Morfontaine with a 62 in 1972. Bordering the vast Ermonsville-Chantilly National Forest, Morfontaine is the most secluded of the clubs in the Paris area, as much a preserve of wild nature as a test of golf.

Like many golfing sites in Europe, St.-Nom-la-Breteche has an intriguing history. Originally a tile factory, then a farm, the property was bought by Louis XIV in 1700 as an extension to his hunting park in Versailles. It remained part of the domain until the Revolution, when it was sold at auction and became a farm again in the hands of its new owners. In 1959, real estate developer Daniel Feau bought the tract and commissioned British golf architect Fred Hawtree to build 36 holes. Almost three centuries after Louis XIV, St.-Nom has reverted to a sporting use for some 1,500 members and their families.

SUMMER

IMPROVEMENT

AS TIME EXPANDS AND GOLF
CONDITIONS REACH PERFECTION,
THE GAME SHIFTS INTO HIGH
GEAR. LESSONS ARE BOOKED,
BUCKETS OF BALLS ARE
SACRIFICED, AND EVERY GOLFER'S
GOAL IS TO GET BETTER.

The golf swing is an athletic event.

—DR. GARY WIREN

Golf and sex are about the only things you can enjoy without being good at it.

—ANONYMOUS

The legendary golf teacher, Harvey Penick of Austin, Texas, still treasures the "little red book" that is the principal source for his best-selling instruction volume. The tattered notebook, containing 60 years' worth of handwritten observations from his busy lesson tee, where Tom Kite and Ben Crenshaw molded their games, makes a powerful impression.

So does studying Ben Hogan's golf grip, as immortalized in bronze in the trophy room at the Colonial Country Club in Fort Worth, Texas. Texas has produced more authentic golf heroes than any other state. Penick, the consummate teaching pro, and Hogan, the consummate playing pro, have been models and inspirations for generations of golfers trying to become more successful at the game.

But curing faults in golf is no easy matter—a little like changing your height long after you've stopped growing. I learned this one day, lying on a couch, listening to the monotonous tick-tock of a metronome and the earnest voice of a shrink who was supposed to be curing my tendency to hit from the top.

"Slowly you turn, slowly you take the club back, slowly you return the club to the ball," lisped the psychiatrist, whose practice consisted largely of helping people overcome more serious addictions and phobias. He was an avid golfer, however—a fact attested to by the practice net in the yard behind his suburban home office and a generous sprinkling of yellow and orange practice balls on his lawn. He honestly believed the European sorcery of Freud, Adler, and Jung applied to a Scottish condition like golf, and he was determined to correct my overly impulsive golf swing with his subliminal suggestions.

Unfortunately, I turned out to be one of those patients who are not susceptible to hypnosis. Instead of falling into the trancelike state where smoking, fear of flying, or a swing tempo could be tackled head on, I fell totally asleep, beyond the psychiatrist's reach, beyond all redemption. "Snoring is not a good sign," he told me on the three occasions we vainly tried the hypnosis cure. And so another great idea for an instruction article went down in flames.

In those days, I was working for a golf magazine. One of my tasks as an underling editor was to elicit pithy swing reminders from teaching pros ("Peel Orange to Escape Sand"), tips from veterans like Paul Runyan ("Pack Honey Snack for Back Nine Attack"), and a three-part lesson series from anyone with even a hunch about what makes a good golf swing. Even now I recall the migraine-inducing series in which a retired Canadian engineer explained the golf swing in terms of Einstein's equation, $E=mc^2$, and then listed a dozen "energy leaks" to avoid in one's own game. I had every one of those energy leaks, and this was before gas prices went up.

If I learned anything at the magazine, it was that golfers are never satisfied with their games, their handicaps, their swings, their putting strokes, or their equipment. They long to improve in all areas. They are particularly susceptible to tips and ideas designed to lengthen their drives. Golf's golden steps, goes the saying, are those paces you take from where your opponent's tee shot has finished in the fairway to where your tee shot has finished in the fairway. This is the macho differential. Women golfers pity us, when they are not scorning us, for being willing to trade a lifetime of short but accurate drives ("Nice shot, Alice") for one humongous John Daly space launch.

hesitate to admit that my own quest for improvement was not much helped by the first-rate instruction I was exposed to in my few years with the golf magazine. The eminent English professional, John Jacobs, showed me how to point the club on my backswing and follow-through. America's superstar teacher of the 1970s, Bob Toski, got me to ratchet down a few degrees my death grip on the club. Davis Love, Jr., the late father of Davis Love III now on tour, memorably impressed me with the role of the imagination in golf, when he invented a shot that took him back to the fairway through a narrow window of opportunity in the woods.

God knows how much money these and other lessons from the playing and teaching professionals on the magazine staff would have cost me if I'd had to pay for them. Of course, I would have asked for my money back because none of them worked. But it wasn't the fault of the sages and gurus. I refused to practice. Golf took long enough as it was. To practice it, too, would have meant skipping meals and giving up family life.

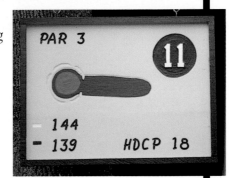

If golfers harbor a belief in the single "secret" that will unlock the mystery of the golf swing for them, they also are vulnerable to an almost superstitious faith in new and different equipment. No one goes through life with just one putter, for instance. Baxter has a new putter in his bag practically every time I play with him. My other golfing friend, De La Farge, is always showing off some new utility club he has just received by mail order. Recently, one of them broke in his hands as he extracted his ball from some heavy rough. The ball flew out, landed and bounced crazily, then rolled on to the green and into the cup for a birdie. When De La Farge went home that day he immediately ordered a new club just like the one that had shattered. Lately, I've been playing with a ball with the "registered" name of Lithium Balata, not because I think it's superior to my Titleists and Top Flites, but because the name itself has a pleasant, narcotic effect on me. Like many golfers facing slightly diminished physical strength, I have also invested in an oversized driver. The miracle club has allowed me to reach certain par-5s in 2, and sometimes, if I am not careful, in 6 or 7.

If you really want to know the effect equipment

has on the game, try depriving a golfer of his favorite couple of clubs for a round. This happened to me in an important money match with Baxter and De La Farge at the end of last summer.

The day before, my brother had passed through town, so I'd taken him for a quick nine holes at my local course, the redoubtable Ashfield Community Golf Club. ("Worst course in the United States," a pro at a neighboring club once had the nerve to tell me.)

At any rate, I'd left my 8-iron—my favorite chipping iron—and my pitching wedge—my stalwart, short-shot surgical tool—alongside the 9th green at the end of my round with my brother, and only discovered they were missing from my bag after I teed off with Baxter and De La Farge at their club on the next day.

From the very first hole at Hickory Ridge, I found myself reaching for the trusty 8-iron or the trusty wedge. Each cruel reminder of their absence sent up my blood pressure, and mental illness swiftly set in. I cursed myself for losing the clubs, and double-cursed the rustic who had probably walked off with them.

On one hole, I tried chipping with my 5-iron,

only to skull the ball. On another hole, I used a sand wedge where normally I would take the pitching wedge, and came up short of the green. "Short of the #$&^%!#$ green!" I said.

It wasn't long before my entire game was feeling the discomfit of the incomplete set. My driving became uneven. Balls began taking unexpectedly bad hops, a sure sign I had got God's goat.

By the time I came to the green on each hole, I was so far out of contention I might as well have been putting with my foot.

Meanwhile, Baxter and De La Farge were having an uncharacteristically fine day for themselves, and would finish 80 and 90, respectively. Both even had a chance to venture into a lower decade on the final green, but missed longish putts. Normally I don't envy other golfers their good luck or great skill, nor do I mind receiving unsolicited advice from them when my own game has gone round the bend. All golfers play on borrowed time, and sooner or later they will get their comeuppance.

ut this day was different. I seethed with a harebrained indignation that is totally out of place on a golf course. I found myself shaking my head vigorously every time Baxter and De La Farge exchanged compliments about each other's shots. "Oh, marvelous, marvelous drive!" said Baxter to De La Farge. "Oh, what a lovely escape from sand!" said De La Farge to Baxter. "Where is the ##$%$&! air sickness bag?" said myself.

It was a beautiful day, so the course was crowded and playing a little slow. There was a twosome behind us, and they were usually putting out on the hole we had just played, as we prepared to do battle on the next one. I was always batting last in our group, owing to the mediocre scores I was posting, and so it began to seem that every time I got set to hit my drive, those two guys would show up.

I don't normally get the jitters when strangers are looking at my golf swing. I'm surprised *they* don't, however. And yet it is a personal matter, the golf swing—not unlike one's signature or chest X-ray, and so I found myself getting irked with our two camp followers. To me, in my weakened condition, they were deliberately showing up in time to see me mangle yet another tee shot. It amused them no end to watch me produce my ghastly salvos. They wore poker faces but laughed within.

At one point I expressed this ridiculous theory to Baxter. On the next tee, he and De La Farge encouraged me to hit first, before the diabolical two-some got there. And so I did, though it violated golfing protocol, and represented abject surrender to my paranoia.

"What a pathetic child I was out there today," I said to my wife that night.

"Maybe you're just coming down with a cold," she replied unhelpfully.

But perhaps she was right. And if the cold turned into pleurisy and pneumonia, so much the better. Baxter and De La Farge would have to visit me in the hospital, and talk to me through the oxygen tent about their most recent golfing successes and how much satisfaction they were getting out of the innocent old game. I went

to bed that night with the Vardon overlapping grip clutching at the very soul.

I slumped through the next day in low spirits, sniffling from time to time with the imaginary cold. In the evening, I phoned Norm Nye, my plumber and spiritual adviser, not to mention former Ashfield Community Golf Club champion, and told him about my missing sticks.

"Why, let me call Stonie, the fellow who rakes the leaves up thair, dontcha know," said Norm. "Somebody will have turned your clubs in to him."

"A likely story," said I, but just a few minutes later, Norm called back.

"Just like I said, somebody handed them in to Stonie," he reported. "He's got your eight-iron and your wedge waiting for you up thair at the clubhouse, as good as new."

I retrieved the missing clubs with mixed feelings. I needed them to complete my arsenal, of course, but having them back gave me two fewer excuses for mis-hits. Still, with all 14 clubs in my bag again, and the fullness of summer before me, I suddenly felt optimistic about my game. Progress was just around the corner, to my way of thinking, if only I made certain small adjustments in my grip, my stance, and my swing. These adjustments had been revealed to me in a dream with the force of prophetic truth that dreams sometimes have.

And so I headed for the driving range to try them out.

Both wood- and steel-shafted clubs manufactured in the 1920s and 1930s (ABOVE) featured head insets designed to catch the eye with designs such as Wright & Ditson's Kro-Flite flying crow. Exotic materials, including ivory, were used for insets, offering the promise of more solid contact and greater distance.

THE BERKSHIRES
The Collectors of Wyantenuck

Golf is a fleeting summer experience in the Berkshires of western Massachusetts, like the music drifting across the meadow at Tanglewood. But collecting golf books and clubs and other golf-related objects of enduring interest is a year-round pursuit, at least for several players with single-digit handicaps at one of the region's oldest clubs, Wyantenuck Country Club in Great Barrington.

At Wyantenuck Golf Club in Great Barrington, Massachusetts, golf collectors are as common as treacherous birdie putts. The random finds of one collector add up to a treasury of golfing miscellany (ABOVE, RIGHT, OPPOSITE, AND FOLLOWING PAGES).

The deceptively short 324-yard 10th hole (ABOVE) at Wyantenuck demands an accurate tee shot because of out-of-bounds on the right and a string of five fairway bunkers on the left, and then a cautious approach to a green that slopes away. The 6,151-yard layout threads through hilly farm country and, for seven holes, the level terrain of an old riverbed.

Golf first came to this town, according to one of those golfers, Jack Dezieck, in the summer of 1895, in the person of a Scotsman named William B. Wight. Taking his clubs along on a visit to his sister, Wight so impressed several locals with his shotmaking, they determined to take up the game themselves. The following year, the group carved out six holes in town and called them Locustwood Golf Club. After two seasons, the club decided it

needed more room and built nine holes along the Housatonic River. The new name for the club, Wyantenuck, meant "bend in the river" in the language of the Mahicanic Indians. This location endured until

Jack Dezieck's pottery collection (OPPOSITE) includes, top row, O'Hara Dial Co. steins made in Paris at the turn of the century and, middle row, Royal Doulton pitchers made in England around 1915. *An ABC of Golf* (RIGHT) was published in 1898 "by a Victim," pseudonym for D. W. C. Falls. Old trophies (BELOW) include the one at left, awarded for Best Net at Wyantenuck Golf Club on July 5, 1909, and the third from left, won by Gertrude J. Leavitt at Wyantenuck on August 20, 1902.

M is for Muscle,
Of which fatty
has piles,
Says he, "I'll just knock it,
A couple o' miles."

1912, when the club commissioned golf architect Robert Pryde of New Haven to build an 18-hole course on some hilly farmland southwest of Great Barrington, and that is where Wyantenuck has remained.

Today, as the club approaches its centenary (along with a neighboring friendly rival, the Stockbridge Golf Club), the past looms into momentary importance, and the collections of the Wyantenuck golfers offer glimpses of the way things used to be. In postcards, trophies, and other artifacts, the early golf of the Berkshires is preserved in distinct regional trappings, as in a handpainted sign announcing the OPENING AND STEAK SUPPER for Lake Garfield Golf Course (no longer in existence), while old clubs, balls, charming ceramic pitchers and mugs, and, above all, books speak to the universal character and appeal of the game.

Roswitha Mott (LEFT) of Great Barrington adds side-stitching to a golf book in distress. Tools of her trade (OPPOSITE) include backing hammer, linen thread, leather, gold leaf, hand tools, and linen tape. The early instruction volume is by J. McAndrew of Cruden Bay, published in Glasgow, circa 1910. Other books in Rusty Mott's extensive collection (RIGHT) include essays by James McHardy, 1895, London, and a 1938 history by Harry Wright, president of the Mexico City Country Club.

Seedbed of Champions

Several decades after he had played intercollegiate golf for Texas A & M, Johnny R. Henry arrived at Austin Country Club to compete in the Trans-Mississippi. Johnny introduced himself to Harvey Penick, longtime golf coach for arch-rival University of Texas, who was helping to run the tournament. Although Henry now sported a beard, Penick had no trouble placing him: "You played down at A & M."

And no wonder he could remember. Henry had defeated one of Penick's top players, Morris Williams, Jr., to help Texas A & M clinch the

At home in Austin, Texas, **Harvey Penick** (LEFT) sits beneath a portrait inscribed to "the greatest instructor the game of golf will ever know." His likeness is etched in glass (ABOVE) at the Austin Country Club, in the club's new location on Lake Austin (BELOW).

1949 Southwest Conference title. That victory was sweet for Henry because Williams was already being touted as the best young golfer of his time, the likely successor to Ben Hogan. In fact, the only college match he ever lost was to Henry, and in the next 12 months, Williams went on to win a kind of Lone Star Slam—the Texas Junior, the Texas Amateur, and the Texas PGA, a feat that has been undupli-cated before or since.

But the recollection also had poignancy because Williams was killed in 1954 when his Air Force F-86 jet crashed on a training mission in Florida, and his extraordinary potential in golf would never be realized.

After graduation, Johnny Henry worked as the greenkeeper at Brookhollow Country Club in Dallas, where he befriended Byron Nelson. In 1975,

The renowned red notebook in which Harvey Penick col-lected, over a period of 60 years, the "images, parables and metaphors that plant in the mind the seeds of shot-making" (RIGHT) was recently transformed into a best-seller (BELOW). On the Austin CC prac-tice tee (BOTTOM), Harvey was still helping golfers at the age of 87.

he was smitten with golf's antiquity on a trip to Scotland, and has since amassed a fine collection of old golf clubs and balls, some of which may be seen in the Magnolia Gas Station he has reclaimed as his shop, under the flag of Texas and a sign that says, simply, JOHNNY R. HENRY, CLUBMAKER.

Explaining why Texas has spawned more than its share of golf champions, some people credit the arid winds and crazy weather; others attribute it to the independent character and positive self-image bred in Texans with long, bumpy cattle drives, big skies, and whatever they put in the barbecue; still

The Colonial Country Club in Fort Worth, Texas (ABOVE LEFT), was the first southern golf course to host the U.S. Open, in 1941. Ben Hogan, who won the inaugural Colonial Tournament, is one of the many top-flight players whose names are recorded on the bronze "Wall of Champions" (LEFT) at Colonial, where practice in tournament management, as in golf (BELOW), has provided the formula for success.

others claim it has to do with the number and variety of homebred role models for anyone taking up the game, from Ben Hogan, Byron Nelson, Jimmy Demaret, Babe Zaharias, and Kathy Whitworth to Lee Trevino, Ben Crenshaw, and Tom Kite.

Then there are the golf courses, spreading even today "like a prairie fire across the vastness of Texas," in the words of Harless Wade, veteran golf writer for the *Dallas Morning Herald*. Colonial, in Fort Worth, built in the 1930s with bent-grass greens—at that time almost unheard of in the South—led the way in winning national recognition for the golf courses of Texas. Colonial's founder, Marvin Leonard, was once praised by Joseph C. Dey, Jr., of the USGA as having "freed the U.S. Open from the East Coast straitjacket in which it had been strapped."

The real-life love story of Valerie and Ben Hogan —Two kids from Texas!

FOLLOW THE SUN

GLENN **FORD** · ANNE **BAXTER** · DENNIS **O'KEEFE**

with JUNE **HAVOC** · LARRY KEATING · ROLAND WINTERS · NANA BRYANT · 20. CENTURY-FOX · Produced by SAMUEL G. **ENGEL** · Directed by SIDNEY **LANFIELD**

Colonial's trophy room is a tribute to Ben Hogan (ABOVE), including a bronze cast (LEFT) of the famous Hogan grip. The movie made of Hogan's life in the 1950s (TOP RIGHT) was long on melodrama, short on the kind of golf that Colonial's 18th green (CENTER RIGHT) has witnessed over the years. Clubmaker and collector Johnny R. Henry (BELOW RIGHT) says "his handshake felt like No. 3 sandpaper."

LONG ISLAND
Traditions Old and New

The rich golfing heritage of Long Island, New York, began when Shinnecock Hills and Maidstone were created in the image of the great old links of Scotland, in 1891, followed by the National Golf Links in 1912, which is "to this day," writes Tom Doak in *Golf in America*, "a wonder for the student of golf architecture."

But no single club on the island evokes the game's past with as much passion and dedication as the Garden City Golf Club, the home course of America's first golf immortal, Walter Travis, and site of America's oldest match-play event. And no club has stirred

Walter Travis (LEFT), the first genuine American golf star, was actually Australian born and did not take up the game until he was 35, making more astounding his U.S. Amateur victories in 1900, 1901, and 1903. Golf course design, including his remodeling of the highly rated Garden City Golf Club on Long Island (ABOVE), was another of Travis's accomplishments.

Both the locker room (OPPOSITE) and reading room (RIGHT) at Garden City reflect the determination of today's members to keep their club in touch with its origins. A recent major renovation to upgrade heating, plumbing, and wiring was accomplished without making the place unrecognizable to "the Old Man," as Walter Travis, the club's patron saint, is affectionately called, even today.

The center-shafted "Schenectady putter," used by Walter Travis to win the 1904 British Amateur is a focal point in a room at Garden City where Travis memorabilia dominate. The putter "performed like a magic wand" over the links at Royal St. George's and prompted the R & A to ban it. When he became the first American to win a major

British golf championship, Travis inspired renewed interest in the game in his adopted homeland. When Garden City began hosting a spring invitation tournament in 1902 for the best amateurs in the country, Travis won it eight years in a row. The Travis Memorial, like the club and the spirit of "the Old Man" at the club, is still going strong today.

as much excitement as the new kid on the block, the Atlantic Golf Club, which could become a new major tournament site on Long Island. The brainchild of real estate developer Lowell M. Schulman, Atlantic GC has a championship layout, designed by Rees Jones on 200 acres of windswept, rough-and-ready farmland. The course is the natural outgrowth of a lifelong enthusiasm for golf on the part of Schulman, whose collection of antique golf-theme ceramics is considered one of the finest in the world.

The Atlantic Golf Club (ABOVE), designed by Rees Jones and opened in 1992, was the brainchild of lifelong golfer Lowell M. Schulman, whose in-house 19th hole (OPPOSITE) attests to a passion for collecting, in this case pottery made in France and Germany in the 1920s.

The Art Deco bronze (LEFT), signed D. Charo, was made in France circa 1925. Decanters (BELOW) with sterling silver appliqué date from the 1920s.

Garden City started in 1897 as a 9-hole course, designed by Devereux Emmet and George Hubbell, and was called the Island Golf Links. It expanded to 18 holes and opened under its present name two years later. The sandy soil, wild grasses, and seaborne winds of the Hempstead Plain were especially well

suited to a golf course in the Scottish style.

Travis came aboard in 1899 and remained active in anything that had to do with the club's golf affairs until his death in 1927. He added pot bunkers to the course, including the one members still call the "Travis bunker," on the left side of the home green. He rebuilt some of the greens to make them more like the putting surfaces he had encountered in Scotland. Not everything he did sat well with fellow members, as when he made the holes on the practice putting green half the size of a standard cup, supposedly to make putting on the course seem easier. But all of them respected his ideas, many of which appeared in the periodical he founded in 1907, *The American Golfer,* and they admired his competitive spirit. "He was always ready to putt you for a cigar," one member recalled, "if you were foolish enough to challenge him and his faithful 'Schenectady.' "

An assortment of gutta-percha and rubber-core balls (OPPOSITE) enjoys an elegant roost in a Royal Doulton bowl by Crombie. The Copeland Spode collection (ABOVE) is from a series in green produced around 1900. A bronze, with a silver patina, of Harry Vardon (FAR LEFT), made by Hal Ludlow in about 1910, contrasts with one of the folksy doorstops (LEFT) that are part of the Schulman collection.

Old vanity license plates (RIGHT) identify the ruling passion of a Down East household. The pro shop and clubhouse (BELOW) of one of Maine's earliest golf clubs are no bigger than they have to be to serve a small summer membership, which prefers substance over style, a characteristic trait of Mainers.

MAINE

Sun, Salt, and Sand Traps

August is the only really busy time for golf at the 100-year-old club that graces one of the islands in Maine's Penobscot Bay. That's when most of the summer members have ferried over with their families to enjoy a few weeks of vacation, and it's when the club schedules most of its tournaments.

But there's nothing frantic in any of this. If you want to play golf, chances are you can just walk up to the first tee, put on your spikes, and tee off. The wildflowers are in the rough. Salt breezes set the flags constantly ablow on the greens. The sharp profiles of sloops and yawls cut nobly across the horizon. Here the passion for golf is often lazy and serene, a change from the pressurized world of the mainland.

It is hard to imagine a place where one's golf score could take on less importance. Doing one's best still matters, of course, but the setting stimulates a philosophy of grace and acceptance. And, as the short, sweet Maine summer evaporates, it is gratifying to know that, for a time, there was perfect peace.

The 9-hole island golf course (RIGHT) radiates from a clubhouse atop the hill down to the waters of Penobscot Bay. In this golf club's summer dining room (TOP RIGHT), the Maine tradition of sailing occupies a place of honor. The bag room (BELOW) is as simply organized as A to Z.

FALL
COMPETITION

SUMMER'S OVER, BUT
COMPETITION HEATS UP ON THE
COURSE, AND NOT EVEN THE
SPECTACLE OF A NEW ENGLAND
AUTUMN CAN TAKE THE EDGE OFF
SUNDAY'S GOLF GAME.

Golf is an exercise which is much used by the Gentlemen in Scotland. A large common, in which there are several little holes, is chosen for the purpose. It is played with little leather balls stuffed with feathers, and sticks tipped with horn. He who putts with the fewest strokes gets the game. . . . A man would live ten years the longer for using this exercise once or twice a week.

—DR. BENJAMIN RUSH, 1770

f any single player personifies the golfer as competitor, surely it is Arnold Palmer, winner of 61 U.S. Tour events between 1955 and 1973. His club, office, and workshop in Latrobe, Pennsylvania, are full of reminders of Palmer's passionate desire to win, both on and off the golf course. Yet his undiminished charisma as a golf star probably has less to do with his winning record over six decades than with his unabashed devotion to the simple traditions of the game. This, too, is palpable at Latrobe.

Golf's spirit of ardent fair play is apparent on the golf course of a small New England college; or in the house of a golf-crazy Atlanta, Georgia, couple; or during the annual hickory-shaft tournament of the Golf Collector's Society, where the entrants don plus fours and long dresses and flail at the ball with mashies and niblicks. Tournaments and matches are the lifeblood of the game at every level.

Every golf club has a reservoir of stories of legendary mishaps and matches that actually took place on its course, and there is always someone, like P. G. Wodehouse's "Oldest Member," on hand to relate them in excruciating detail at the drop of an innocent question.

Years ago, one hapless visitor to Pine Valley Golf Club in New Jersey, "the toughest golf course in the world," according to Herbert Warren Wind, made a

43 on the par-3 14th hole and swiftly entered club annals. A memorable match at the same club involved a member and his guest, the broadcaster John Daly (not to be confused with the long-hitting PGA champion of the same name). Daly was a poor golfer, the sort Pine Valley devours for an appetizer, so the member bet him he couldn't win all 18 holes even if he was given a generous seven shots a hole. The match began. With his huge advantage, Daly held his own until he ran into trouble on 15. At the moment of truth, he was on the green in 11, 40 feet from the hole. But his opponent was on the green in 3, only 15 feet away.

The world-weary golf observer will know exactly what happened next. Against all odds, Daly sank the 40-footer. The member, unnerved, 3-putted for 6, losing to Daly's 12. And the underdog won the last three holes and the bet.

Some tournaments are devised for novelty's sake—playing a course backwards from green to tee; or playing at night, in the light of a full moon; or tossing back a shot of Scotch after every shot of golf (an event played every year at a club in England, in which no participant has yet made it past the 10th hole). There are tournaments for left-handers, professional football players, country music performers, tax attorneys, uniformed policemen, and every age group from 10-and-under to 80-and-over. One annual tournament in this country is limited to teams of players from clubs founded at least 100 years ago. Most of these events are necessarily more social than competitive, with team formats that take the sting out of failure and loss.

Then there is the real McCoy. When Bobby Jones retired from "the neurological nightmare of championship golf," he offered an important distinction. "There are two kinds of golf, and they are worlds apart," Jones declared. "There is the game of golf, and there is tournament golf."

Until players get used to it, which most don't, tournament golf at the highest level—which is to say walking down the 15th or 16th fairway with a slim lead in a major championship—produces indigestion, ulcers, nausea, hyperventilation, and temporary blindness.

Jack Nicklaus has succeeded in overcoming the inhuman pressures of championship golf with such frequency and grace that his unsurpassed career may be said to be the exception that proves the rule.

As Alistair Cooke wrote, long before Nicklaus washed his hands of winning major titles, "He is probably the only great golfer alive—or dead—who could honestly have meant what he said to an English friend who casually asked him what his idea was of the most rousing prospect in golf. 'Three holes to go, and you need two pars and a birdie to win.'"

When Dr. Rush, the surgeon-general of the American Revolution, published his "sermon to the rich and studious" in Philadelphia, it was the first written mention of golf on this continent. It went to the core of things in defining golf as competition. "He who putts with the fewest strokes gets the game" sums up the major titles as well as anything. And it established the notion that golf is an exercise, which some call a canard of the first order.

Anyone who has walked 18 holes after a bit of a layoff knows there is at least some exercise value in a round of golf. You may not come up lame and halting, as you might after three sets of tennis singles, but your legs will register the rigors of four or five miles of walking, some of it uphill, sideways, or in deep sand, and your hand-me-down gout might kick in, too.

Counting practice swings and mulligans, the average 100-shooter probably exerts as much energy in a round as, say, the farmer haying five acres with his lofted scythe.

On the other hand, no one pretends golf breeds peak cardiovascular fitness, especially when it is played, as many Americans play it, from a moving vehicle. Most Europeans carry their own bags, or use trolleys to wheel the bags around. To rub it in, they generally walk 18 holes faster than we ride them. I won't soon forget the day, playing by myself on a modest, off-the-beaten-path course in Scotland, I had to cede way to two middle-aged women playing at an amazingly sprightly pace behind me, with their Westies in tow. The dogs yapped at me with fairly obvious disdain as they passed.

Yet today's top players, exercising in order to better compete, acknowledge that fitness can contribute to performance. "Fifteen years ago, golfers didn't take care of themselves as athletes," Jack Nicklaus observed after he and fellow oldsters Arnold Palmer, Gary Player, and Ray Floyd posted stellar opening rounds in a recent Masters Tournament. Nicklaus claimed his daily exercise regimen had helped prepare him for becoming the oldest player ever to hold the lead in the Masters. "If I can win at forty-six," he said, referring to his emotional victory at Augusta

National in 1986, "I can win at fifty-three."

The competitive gene does not diminish with age, but it begins to need help around about 50. In a classic case of age outsmarting biology, Arthur Rubenstein gave the illusion of playing the piano faster than he really was by introducing more ritardandos at slackened pace before fast segments in the pieces he performed. The result was that his playing speed sounded livelier than it really was, and his music came across as young and as vital as ever.

The ritardando gambit can and should be used in golf to thwart the young champion ("YC"). This strategy might be summed up as follows:

In a match, insist on walking rather than taking a golf cart.

On the front 9, walk at a leisurely (but not slow) pace between shots, to make certain YC, riding his golf cart, is kept waiting ahead of you in the fairway on every hole. This will disrupt his concentration, stiffen his back muscles, and cause negative swing images to fill his mind.

On the back 9 (after secretly fortifying yourself with a tablespoon of honey), pick up the pace so that you are in a position to be waiting for him to shoot. This will not be hard to do, for YC subconsciously will have begun to dawdle so as not to be so far ahead of you, and by now, his tempo no longer intact, he will be taking more shots on every hole, anyway.

Wait for a crucial swing hole to pull out all stops. When YC hooks his tee shot into the woods on No. 17, make sure your drive lands in the fairway. While YC stomps among the lodgepole pines, quickly play your second shot, a nifty 5-wood to the elevated green. Then walk double-time to the green.

The idea is to be pacing back and forth on the green with your putter conspicuously on your shoulder, while YC, having been forced to play his second shot sideways back into the fairway, is addressing his third shot with a long iron.

If your distracting and pestiferous presence in his field of vision does not cause him to dump the next shot into a greenside bunker, by the time he races up to the green he will be in poor form for the art of putting. You will have got your breath back (barely) and the possibility of 3-putting will not occur to you.

You win the hole and, 2 up with 1 to play, the match.

Alas, I do not have a competitive makeup, having lost it during a bout with scarlet fever as a lad. But this does not mean I fail to recognize and appreciate it when I see it, particularly among the golfers who are always winning money off me.

Baxter is such a competitor that he will make bets on who's got the better practice swing. He is a natural medal-play man, keeping track of every stroke, always measuring himself against the haughty perfection of the card. The higher mathematics of the bottom line are his calling. He keeps few of his internal musings to himself on a golf course.

On 2 tee: "A bogey on one. Not an auspicious start."

On 2 green: "Another bogey. This is a disaster."

After a good drive on 6: "I'm two over after five, but if I par out, making the bird on nine, I'll be only one over at the turn."

After 3-putting 9: "These greens suck, I'll never break eighty now."

On 15 tee, after his first birdie: "I need to finish par-birdie-par-birdie for a decent score."

On 15 tee, after hitting his drive out-of-bounds: "I hate this game."

On 18 tee, after two consecutive pars: "I have to play for pars, like the pros do in the Open. I can only take what the course will give me."

On 18 green, after his par gave him an 86: "What time do you want to play tomorrow?"

 axter's competitiveness is what gives a raw, delicious edge to his temper and the splendid arc to his occasional javelin throw, usually with the driver or putter. Then he becomes so ashamed and remorseful that for several holes he is a disappointing conversationalist. But he always snaps out of it.

There is no risk of injury playing with Baxter, by the way, because you always know when he's about to throw something. It's when he starts whistling.

Head-to-head match play is De La Farge's game. This is the man you would trust with your life, such is his kindness and integrity, his compassion, his gracious bearing in any circumstance—not to mention what Baxter calls his "essential wierdness." De La Farge is apt to spring on his playing companions such esoteric stumpers as, "Did you hear what Lord Byron said when he spilled hot tea on his lap?" Baxter likes to tell me, "De La Farge is the smartest fellow I've ever played golf with," adding pointedly, "present company not excepted."

Yet in a match De La Farge is a killer, tenacious and lion-hearted. "The Geneva Convention doesn't apply to golf," he once remarked after making an opponent play a 15-inch putt. The opponent missed.

The unplayable lie is not in De La Farge's vocabulary, at least not when he is in an important match. I have seen him play shots out of oak trees, rocky streams, lava pits, sacred burial grounds, rattlesnake nests, and ladies' rooms. Once, paired with him in a better ball match, I made the mistake of suggesting we pick up instead of trying to play a shot that had landed in two feet of standing rainwater on the side of the fairway.

"Are you insane?" he lashed out at me, ripping off his golf shoes and rolling up his trousers. "We're still in this!" And he actually played a terrific 6-iron to the green, spattering me with mud and grass, for good measure, on his followthrough.

De La Farge is the first to admit he has difficulty seeing, especially long distances, and Baxter and I make it a point to get a fix on his ball as well as on our own, especially off the tee. Like all of us, De La Farge has produced some beauteous mishits, but, thanks to his limited vision, his face always looks serene when he finishes a stroke. And why shouldn't it—he can't see the damage he's done.

If I have learned anything from De La Farge, it is to adopt his mask of composure following every shot. Perhaps I would have come to this pretty pass with yoga or Zen. But as it happened, I obtained my philosophy of life directly from De La Farge, and I am grateful.

Duck at the whistle. Smile on the followthrough. Make judicious use of the ritardando gambit. In the fall, invoke the leaf rule.

The passionate golfer could do worse.

TOURNAMENTS
Countrified, Collegiate, and International

The season at Northfield Golf Club in the rural countryside of Massachusetts starts with a Scramble in the spring and finishes with the Mixed Scotch Foursomes in the fall. In between, there's the Northfield Cup and the Northfield Open, and the Member-Member and the Member-Guest, and the crown jewel, the Club Championship. And those are but a few of the events on the yearly tournament schedule.

Northfield Golf Club (ABOVE AND BELOW), the last remnant of a summer resort hotel that thrived at the turn of the century, enjoys renewed prosperity with an active local membership and daily fee players over its wooded 9-hole layout.

The same is true at every other golf club, whether it's ultraprivate, semipublic, ultrapublic, military, civilian, or semiserious. The Company of Gentlemen Golfers in Leith devised the first rules of golf in 1744 and a few minutes later were busy recording the first challenge matches in their "bett book." There has always been action on the golf course, with money and honor in varying amounts riding on just about every shot. The constant pressure in a match is what led Ring Lardner to declare, "The easiest shots in golf are the fourth putt and the explosion shot off the tee." It's also probably behind the recent report from the

In Northfield's no-frills clubhouse (OPPOSITE), the locker rooms are identified by images hand-painted by an artistic member in the early 1950s. The male golfer resembles the young Ben Hogan, when his stance was wider than his shoulders and he was still afflicted with a hook. The female golfer appears modeled after Babe Didrikson Zaharias in her prime.

Ministry of Health in Tokyo that asserts golf is more likely to kill a Japanese man over 60 than tennis, running, or climbing Mount Fuji.

But one of the great strengths and appeals of the game is its infinite variety of competitive formats. Of course, things don't always pan out for would-be champions, as sporting artist A. B. Frost observed in his turn-of-the-century golfing alphabet:

G is the game we expected to play,
But which didn't come off on the tournament day.

Northfield was built as part of a summer hotel compound in a period around the turn of the century when fashionable golf was spreading to holiday resort areas almost as fast as the starched collar and the supper dansant. Cape Cod, the lakes and islands of Maine, the Adirondacks, the Green and White mountains of New England, the Jersey Shore, and any spa town ending in the word "Springs" jumped onto the golfing bandwagon. The mayor of Austin, Texas, discovered golf at one of the new enclaves on Cape Cod and returned home to build Hancock Golf Club, the first course in Texas. This was also the time when Californians got their first taste of golf in areas that have since become almost synonymous with golf and with notable tournament sites: San

Taconic Golf Club, the home course of the Williams College golf team, was designed by Wayne Stiles, "the most overlooked golf architectural genius in history," according to Massachusetts-based golf-course architect and historian Geoffrey Cornish. The club is regarded as having one of the greatest courses of the 1920s. Its vintage is evident in the trophies in the clubhouse (LEFT) and in the portraits of Ephmen golf teams (OPPOSITE), which delineate eras of fashion in apparel and hair style, as well as golf equipment.

Diego County and Monterey Peninsula.

Around the same time, starting with the Ivy League schools, colleges and universities took up golf as a fall sport and a great new way to spend Mater and Pater's money. On the wall next to the bar at the Taconic Golf Club, the home course of Williams College, in Williamstown, Massachusetts, there are photographs of the golf teams from 1904 to 1980. The pictures show that collegiate golfers wore argyles and plus fours in the 1920s, white bucks and crewcuts in the 1940s, and long hair and jeans in the 1970s;

At St.-Germain Golf Club (LEFT), near Paris, upcoming club competitions are posted on a slate blackboard. The diagram for the 520-yard 15th hole (FAR LEFT) bears the club emblem. Originally formed in 1890 as Golf de l'Ermitage in the city, St.-Germain still conveys the ambience of a French café in its terraces (BELOW).

nowhere is it given which outfit worked the best on the golf course.

Taconic hosted the NCAA National Championship in 1958, when Phil Rodgers of the University of Houston won the title. Besides Rodgers, entrants in the field that year who went on to successful careers as tour pros were Tommy Aaron, Al Geiberger, Don Massengale, and

The first tee at St.-Germain (BELOW) offers a glimpse of the relatively flat, tree-lined, and well-bunkered course designed by British golf architect Henry Colt in 1922. Although the award presentation photo from the club's early days (LEFT) hardly suggests a winner-take-all mentality, the competitive juices flow among today's members (ABOVE) just as soon as spikes are on and bags are lashed to their pull carts.

COLLECTORS
Riches of the Game

Wayne Aaron was fighting gloom. Lying on his back in the doctor's office to receive therapy for a torn rotor muscle, he was facing the prospect of giving up golf because of the injury. Then another patient casually mentioned having stopped, on his way to the clinic, to investigate some old golf clubs and a suitcase sticking out of a trash can. "He'd retrieved the suitcase," Wayne recalls, "but left the clubs behind because they looked unplayable—he told me one even had holes in its shaft, as if that made it really useless.

"I raised straight up off the bed, found out where the trash can was located, cut my therapy session short, and made a mad dash for it," he relates. "Miracle of miracles, the clubs were still there, and in the middle of twelve wood-shafted irons and woods was exactly what I had hoped to find—the finest Spalding Golf Medal mashie you have

Among the storied treasures in the Aaron house (ABOVE) is the Corby Challenge Cup (BELOW), made by Royal Doulton-Lambeth for Molesey Hurst Golf Club in England in 1912. The ceramic trophy with silver medallions encircling its base was awarded to the winners of a tournament played among top amateur golfers from England, Wales, Scotland, and Ireland.

The collection of Wayne and Claudia Aaron includes (OPPOSITE) a 1930s table lamp made of pot metal, depicting two women on a park bench observing a male golfer. Avid golfers as well as collectors, the Aarons live a few steps away from their home course (BELOW), Cherokee Town and Country Club in Atlanta.

A rare Royal Worcester porcelain cup and saucer set (OPPOSITE), each piece depicting a different hole at Gleneagles, Scotland, was hand-painted and signed by R. Rushton around 1900. The Owens Utopian Golf Vase (BELOW), a remarkable example of slip-painted underglaze decorated artware, was introduced in 1897 by John B. Owens Pottery Company, Zanesville, Ohio.

Golf scenes, hand-painted and sgraffitoed, decorate Weller Dickensware pottery (ABOVE) made between 1897 and 1905. A rare Morrisian Ware jardiniere (BELOW), 16 inches tall and 18 inches across, decorated with Bradley-style golf figures, was made by Royal Doulton around 1900. Next to it, on the tee, is an early 1900s wood carving by French sculptor Vincent André Becquerel.

ever seen, with a patented Laird metal shaft, holes and all."

So much for Wayne Aaron's gloom. That find not only added a specimen club to his extensive collection but "speeded up my recovery more than any help I was receiving at the clinic," he recalls, so that he was soon playing golf again.

The Atlanta, Georgia, businessman and his wife, Claudia, have been collectors throughout their now 31-year marriage, beginning with American antiques such as clocks, Depression glass, and country store primitives. Even their three sons got in the act, growing up. "We always took them with us to the flea markets and farm sales," Claudia recalls, and each boy developed a collecting passion of his own, from lead soldiers to Navy ship models.

The Aarons were introduced to "the world of golf antiquity" when they stumbled on the Old Golf Shop in Cincinnati, Ohio. Later encounters with noted golf collectors Joe Murdoch, Robert Kuntz, and, especially, Ray Davis, inspired the couple to begin a collection of their own.

Today, Wayne and Claudia have one of the largest and most beautiful collections of golf ceramics, glass, and silver in the world—as well as that funny metal club with the holes in it.

Next to a Flo-blue-style porcelain vase made in 1910 (FAR LEFT) are three examples of Royal Doulton Burslem, made between 1885 and 1902. Above the Czech-made cocktail shaker and glasses (ABOVE LEFT) is a silver belt buckle awarded by Cheltenham Golf Club in 1898. The sterling silver spoons (ABOVE RIGHT) date from the turn of the century. The countertop papier-mâché advertising figures (BELOW) were used to promote the superiority of the Silver King golf ball in the late 1800s.

An alcove full of early golf equipment, from fringe mowers to hole cutters, includes old clubs displayed in a country-store broom stand and, leaning against the opposite wall, a club claimed as one of the oldest in existence, dating from 1640. "Indoor Golf," made in 1921, features Tommy Green and Sissy Lofter—miniature figures manipulated by pressing a trigger on the shaft of a full-size club.

Early long-nose wood "play clubs" and four early irons on the wall date from 1780 to 1860, and represent most of the early Scottish club makers, including Tom Morris, Willie Park, Sr., Robert Forgan, and Willie Dunn. Turn-of-the-century patented clubs are displayed in an antique umbrella stand. The display case holds early feather and gutty balls, ball molds, golf medals, caddie badges, scoring devices, unusual tees, sand tee molds, early books, and other items related to the formative years in the game of golf.

TRADITIONS
Hickory Hackers Open

The tournament is played every year, usually in conjunction with the annual convention of the Golf Collectors' Society of America. When it was held at Bobby Jones's home course, East Lake Country Club in Atlanta, Georgia, a man in kilts serenaded the groups with bagpipes as they teed off. There is an art to playing with the wood-shafted clubs that were the tools of the golfer's trade prior to the 1930s, when steel came in. "You must swing more slowly," says Johnny R. Henry, who won the Hickory Hackers Open in 1978. "If you try to swing these clubs with the modern tempo and leg drive," he says, "you'll hit the ball forty-five degrees off line." He figures he loses 20 to 25 yards off the tee with his antique drivers, and needs one club more than his

usual selection when he plays an iron. Henry started in the game with wood-shafted clubs, receiving his first set of Spalding juvenile hickories in 1933, when he was a kid. The year he won the Open, entrants were limited to seven clubs, so he carried a brassie, a mid-mashie, a mashie, a mashie-niblick, a niblick, a wedge, and a Ray Mills aluminum putter. Now players can carry as many clubs as they want, including the deep-grooved irons that are illegal under today's rules, because that's the way it was in Jones's day.

Tournaments played with wood-shafted clubs are popular with traditionalists, especially golf collectors who have old clubs and want to find out how they perform. Images collected at the Hickory Hackers Tournament (on these and following pages) at East Lake Country Club, Atlanta, Georgia, show it is possible for onlookers and participants alike to step back into golfing time for an afternoon.

Arnold Palmer, president of Latrobe Country Club (ABOVE AND BELOW) in western Pennsylvania, and an important local figure, is as popular in his hometown today as he was when he first arrived on the national golf scene in 1954 to win the U.S. Amateur tournament.

HEROES
Arnold Palmer at Latrobe

When the greenkeeper's son grows up to buy the club, it makes a good story, especially in a working man's town like Latrobe, Pennsylvania, where hard-won success is the only success worth toasting (with a locally brewed Rolling Rock beer).

Milfred J. Palmer, nicknamed "Deacon," took the golf course superintendent's job at Latrobe Country Club in 1912. By the time Arnold, the first of his four children, was born in 1919, Deacon was also serving as the golf professional. The young

In a lounge in the clubhouse, a portrait, given by members of Cherry Hills Country Club in Denver, shows a victorious Palmer on the final hole of the 1960 U.S. Open. His closing 65 at Cherry Hills made up a seven-shot deficit and set a pattern for the come-from-behind victories that electrified galleries and made Arnie the first and most influential golf hero of the television age. The bronze made by Royal McCullough in 1986 captures Palmer's signature finish.

Dr. Arnold D. Palmer Esquire

DOCTOR OF LAWS
MAKES EM & BREAKS EM
[HAN]DLES ANYTHING
HOUSE CALLS·

[E]asy

of golf that
Two such
face, such
r off pine
I is not so
nately 30
d stance
s or any
 oad into
select a
a chip
e club
oulder
st im-
must
e can
pos-
left at

...your ball is precariously
...needles or twigs you must be extremely
...b. First be careful when placing your club behind the
ball, if you disturb the lie, the ball is apt to move resulting in
a penalty stroke. The better choice is to place the clubface
behind the ball with the sole of the club slightly off the ground
I then hit the spot with the same technique as mentioned before, making certain I strike the ball first and the twigs or pine-
needle last.

Half blast from a sandy lie

One of the most difficult shots to handle
around the green is the sandy lie. Specifically
this is a lie in the rough where the ball is
lying on a combination of soft sand and tufts
of grass. If you could hit a full shot from this
lie there would be no problem, but when you
need to carry the ball just a few yards over a
hazard to a tough pin placement, you've got
trouble. The danger is, if you hit just a fraction behind the ball, you'll never make the
green, and if you swing full and take little or
no sand there's a good chance you'll skull
the ball — the latter being a result of the
flange bouncing off the sand and grass into
the ball. After years of competitive play, in
which I encountered this shot numerous
times, I found the "half blast shot" to be the
most successful. The technique I use is very
similar to a trap shot. If the ball is sitting
well, use your sand blaster. Play the ball more
toward your left heel, with your weight concentrated on your left side. Take the club
back half-way, a little beyond waist high.
Make sure you take a little sand behind the
ball, how much depends on the texture of the
sand and what is below the immediate surface. The fact that you're not in a hazard
gives you the opportunity of grounding your
club. How your club sets at the ball can
reveal the nature of your lie. I can't over-
emphasize hitting through the ball — don't
quit at the ball — hit it firmly and finish. To
overcome your fear of this shot, you must
practice for feel and accuracy.

All material from GOLF magazine

Tough lies m[ust]

There are lies you must deal
ordinarily would drive you to the
lies that come to mind are the sh
as a road or off clay, and the de
needles or twigs. In the first case
difficult as it looks. Let's assume
yards from the green on a road.
you would use a pitching wedge.
other club is that the flange will k
the ball causing a top or a skull.
four or five iron—assume the sta
shot, and concentrate on the ba
back without breaking the wrists
to turn slightly, under and towar
portant phase of this shot is co
meet the back of the ball first, ti
strike the road—with no detrime
sible don't allow your right ha
impact—keep the blade square.
sitting on a bed of pine-needles o
cautious. First be careful when
ball, if you disturb the lie, the b
a penalty stroke. The better ch
behind the ball with the sole of t
I then hit the spot with the same
making certain I strike the b
last.

Hand action[on]
short pitches

I hit the shot with little or
no hand action. To accomplish this I draw
the club back with very little wrist break, letting my shoulders take the club back. From
a half to three-quarter swing (depending on
the distance), I turn my shoulder into the

[chip]ch from the short rough

How many times have you hit a great shot to a pin only
to have the ball hit and skid over the back of the green

Palmer was forbidden to play with members' children or to swim in the club pool, but Deacon let him on the course when it was empty, early and late in the day. From the age of seven, Arnold was consumed by the game.

Almost six decades, eight major championships, and more than 70 U.S. and Senior Tour titles later, Palmer still was consumed by the game. His devotion to golf transcended the fiery competitive spirit he brought to it. Just as his father's early admonition to hit the ball hard produced the patented wrenching torque of the Palmer swing, the solitary rounds of Palmer's youth, like stolen pleasures, revealed to him the delicious complexity of the challenge of man against course, and taught him the values of sportsmanship and integrity prized by traditional boosters of the game.

At Latrobe, the King's mementos range from tournament trophies (ABOVE) to a line of wallpaper that infiltrated dens and offices across America with Palmer's swing tips (OPPOSITE). The plaque was a joke gift after Wake Forest awarded Palmer an honorary degree in 1970. The photograph of Arnold's father (INSET, OPPOSITE) hangs over the locker, now permanently closed, used by "Deacon" until his death in 1976, along with a 1961 photo of a foursome consisting of "Deacon," Arnold, Gary Player, and "Old Har"—club president Harry S. Saxman.

But it was his style of play that won the heart of the golfing public, as when he drove the green on the par-4 first hole in the fourth round of the 1960 U.S. Open at Cherry Hills. As Peter Andrews described the Palmer style in *Golf Digest,* "We cannot play his game, but he plays ours. . . . For most of us to gaze upon the silken grace of a Sam Snead was to know that we could no more play golf well than we could join the Ballet Russes. But Palmer's swing, looking like the sort of thing you would expect to see from a member of the riot squad putting down a street demonstration, we could understand. Palmer always included us in his round."

Latrobe Country Club reflects the tastes and values of its owner, as in traditional table settings (LEFT) in the dining room and voluminous samples of golf weaponry in the workshop (RIGHT). The trophies in Palmer's office (BELOW) include a tribute to his acing the par-3 2nd hole at the TPC at Avenel, Potomac, Maryland, with a 5-iron on consecutive days in 1988, in pro-ams of the inaugural Chrysler Cup Matches.

HISTORIAN
A Scotsman in America

In contrast to Arnold Palmer's informal approach to collecting, Alastair Johnston has gone about it in a deliberate, focused, and highly proficient manner. Johnston—Palmer's friend, neighbor in Bay Hill, Florida, and senior vice president of Arnold Palmer Enterprises—has put together a library of nearly 7,000 volumes, the most extensive collection of golf literature in private hands in the world.

The native Scotsman is probably as competitive about books as Palmer is about golf. But his library is not about books as trophies, or collecting for collecting's sake. More than a hobby, it represents a passionate attempt to create "a coordinated perspective of golf's adoption as a national sport." In acquiring

PROGRAM

National Open Golf Championship
SCIOTO COUNTRY CLUB. COLUMBUS. O.
JULY 8, 9, 10.

One wall in the world's largest private golf library (RIGHT) pays heed to one of the game's classic eras with the swings of Ted Ray, J. H. Taylor, Harry Vardon, and James Braid, and a group portrait, *The Scottish Bench and Bar,* 1890. Below is a long spoon, made by Willie Park in 1895, and used by John Inglis, Chief Justice of Scotland, former captain of the R & A, and playing partner and mentor to Young Tom Morris. Inglis delivered Young Tom's eulogy when Morris died in 1875 at the age of 24. Fictional deaths on the golf course are recorded in mysteries dating from 1902 (OPPOSITE), while a U.S. Open program (ABOVE) from 1926, the year Bobby Jones won his second Open, captures the winning style of the "golden age of sport."

the rare antiquarian titles and other documents in his collection, Johnston was motivated by a desire to verify the story of golf for the centuries that, until now, he believes, had remained largely in the dark ages of surmise and speculation.

Specifically, Johnston has searched the period from 1457, when golf was first mentioned in *The Lawes and Acts of Parliament*, to 1857, when the first general text on golf, *The Golfer's Manual*, appeared.

After eight years of research, he and his father, James F. Johnston, have published the findings in *The Chronicles of Golf: 1457 to 1857*, a monumental volume of 734 pages.

"While the book necessarily focuses on

Scotland as being 'the cradle of golf' since the 15th century," the authors write, "significant attention is devoted to the spread of the game to England and Ireland, as well as the colonies of North America, India, and Australia. By the middle of the 19th century, no frontier had been found insurmountable, and around the globe, in any given open terrain, the click of clubhead on gutta ball became an increasingly familiar echo."

Golf has spread into many languages, most notably Japanese (LEFT), since January 31, 1682, the date of a rare letter (ABOVE LEFT) owned by Alastair Johnston, in which the Duke of York, later King James II, describes "playing at Goffe." An eight-year research project on Johnston's desk (ABOVE) has produced a book that traces the development of golf in Scotland since 1457. After years of attending the Masters every spring, Johnston has concluded that a current clubhouse badge for Augusta during tournament week, "the hottest ticket in sports," is probably as valuable as one of the rare early Masters programs in his collection (OPPOSITE).

WINTER
R E M E M B R A N C E

WHEN COLD WEATHER FORCES A
STRATEGIC RETREAT FROM THE
GAME, THE GOLFER TURNS TO THE
THREE R'S—READING, REFLECTION,
AND RESORTS.

Gentlemen with large handicaps are requested to play long holes from the Ladies Tees.

—BYE LAW NO. 16, BOURNE GOLF CLUB, APRIL 1, 1874

G olf is played in society. The basic social unit is the foursome. When it is winter, the foursome goes south. In the case of Baxter, De La Farge, Squinty, and the undersigned, it goes to Pinehurst, North Carolina, picking the one week it rained every day. But it was a warm rain, and we were grateful. We played Pinehurst No. 1, No. 4, No. 5, No. 7, and, on our last day, the famous No. 2. Baxter and I shared an outspoken caddie named Eddie. Before we finished the first hole, Eddie had been outspoken on my grip, my stance, and what he called my "faulty swing shift." Needless to say, I played the championship Donald Ross design like a chump that day. Then we came home, and didn't see each other again until spring.

Pinehurst, by the way, was America's first genuine golf resort. It became the prototype for the development of southern destinations for northern golfers in winter that continues to this day with a vengeance. If you can't go south, you can dream about it. Such settings as the paneled library of the PGA National Hall of Fame and the antique-filled den and library of master teaching professional Gary Wiren could get the armchair golfer through many snowbound Sundays in style.

Or you can hasten spring by planning the ultimate golf trip, a journey to Scotland. But if you go, don't rub it in on your less fortunate golfing buddies, as De La Farge and Squinty did when

they shot over to St. Andrews for a long weekend a couple of years ago. They telephoned from the bar in Rusack's and gave me a blow-by-blow account of their adventures across the Old Course—as if I cared how many shots it took Squinty to escape from the bunker called Devil's Asshole.

I have not mentioned Squinty until now, because he has not been a regular member of the foursome of late. His wife, you see, has taken up the game again, and Squinty plays with her. Baxter, De La Farge, and I have been meaning to discuss this ticklish issue with Squinty, but we haven't gotten around to it. The truth is, our foursome is damned if we do and damned if we don't.

Because when Eve has entered the garden and stands on the tee with her apple, a 90-compression Blue Dot, in her hand, there is trouble ahead.

The sexes seldom mingle harmoniously on the golf course, for reasons best not explored here. That helps to explain why, on the historic links of Aberdeen, one of the birthplaces of the game, there is the Royal Aberdeen Golf Club, on one side, and the Aberdeen Ladies' Golf Club, on the other. That is the way it has been since time immemorial. Ben

and Valerie Hogan do not play together. Jack and Barbara Nicklaus do not play together. Old Tom Morris and Mrs. Morris do not play together.

So it was my rare privilege to play in a mixed foursome over a period of time that revealed both the promise and the futility of forcing the sexes together on the golfsward.

We were not a jolly foursome, but the circumstance of marriage threw us together two or three times a year, usually at birthdays and holidays, for a few rounds. Like customer golf, family golf can be played for profit or for loss. It all depends on the personalities involved.

ietrich Mosel, my father-in-law at the time, was a small, formal man of German extraction, loyalty, and temperament. He was one of those rare self-taught golfers whose swing actually looked sound, not like a Rube Goldberg invention. Dietrich loved the game but seemed ill at ease in it, accepting its punishing vagaries with a characteristic smirk. He wore wire-rimmed glasses, smoked Camels, quoted from Spengler's *Decline of the West,* and always picked up the check. With his custom-fitted clubs, and, inside his wallet, four crumpled swing tips from an early issue of *Golf Digest,* he had played to as low as 7 or 8, but in the years I knew Dietrich, his short game had begun to fall apart. I couldn't watch him on the greens. The crosshanded grip he'd adopted did nothing to stave off his yips. Anything inside of 4 feet was slippery work, and the look on his face whenever he missed was pure existential despair.

Mike Brennan, my brother-in-law, was a former minor league catcher with Popeye arms, hyperthyroid eyes, and a melancholy Irish nature. He was

left-handed, had a 15 or 16 handicap, and stood up to the ball deep in the box, with murder in his heart. His stiff-shafted forged irons were so heavy they could have been used to hold up a suspension bridge. If he had the honor, I made it a point to study cloud formations. Otherwise, the furious way he went about teeing off would affect my swing motion and I'd produce an exaggerated slice.

Then there was Leslie, maiden name Mosel (which she reassumed after our marriage). Leslie had a long, flowing golf swing that put the rest of us to shame. She routinely outdrove us, even without an advantage on ladies' tees. She couldn't putt any better than her father—not because of her nerves but out of lack of interest. Putting bored her. She frittered away strokes around the green with such regularity that, on the card at the round's end, Leslie and I always ended up neighbors in the 90s. But this did not fool me, or anyone else who watched us play. Leslie was the golfer.

I used to think of her as one of those winsome female characters in P. G. Wodehouse's golf stories, who goes out and wins the club championship and the heart of the richest, handsomest member at the same time. If you caught sight of Leslie from another fairway, you might assume she was on holiday from the LPGA tour, or at least a ranking amateur. Her full swing was so athletic and well-grooved that club pros would point her out to their pupils. Chewing on a tee between shots and balancing a club on her

shoulder, she strode the fairways with the lazy confidence of a Tom Weiskopf. Unlike Weiskopf, she usually wore culottes when she played, and kept her long, auburn hair in a ponytail.

Leslie inherited her talent and beauty from her mother, a former Western Junior champion who, after divorcing Dietrich when Leslie and her baby sister, Linda, were still small, left Chicago and married a Jaguar dealer in Fort Worth. The arrangement was for the girls to live with the mother during the school year, with the father during the summer. So Leslie grew up playing the game at South Shore CC in Chicago with her father, and at Colonial CC in Fort Worth with her mother. In Fort Worth she'd seen Babe Zaharias play and she'd met Ben Hogan. *She'd met Ben Hogan!*

By the time I entered the picture, we would play together either at South Shore or at Wykagyl, Mike's home club in New Rochelle, New York, and, on winter breaks, at John D. MacArthur's PGA National in Palm Beach Gardens. These were rich and tony venues for my blood. I had recently landed a job on a golf magazine, but it gave me nothing like the exposure to the country club way of life that marriage did.

If anything, business trips I made for the magazine armed me with the wrong tools for genteel golfing society. For example, in the wake of Orville Moody's U.S. Open victory in 1969, I watched the great Enlisted Man perform various trick shots during a round he played for the media at La Costa in California. The following weekend, I attempted to duplicate one of the shots for my brother-in-law on the practice tee at Wykagyl, using his left-handed 1-iron. The Sarge had taken out a flock of birds with the shot he played. I hit a screamer through the French doors of a fourth-floor apartment overlooking the golf course with mine.

"Let's go hit a few putts," said Mike after the sound of shattering glass brought activities on the practice tee to a respectful halt.

My appreciation of the solace found in the dark, clubby interiors of a male sanctuary dated from this time. I enjoyed lolling around the old locker room at storied Wykagyl after a round, with its clangy metal lockers, long, spike-marked benches, and mammoth porcelain urinals. While Dietrich and Mike suited up for the ritual drinks and dinner with "the girls," I'd be helping myself to the talc and Witch Hazel and shooting the breeze with the guy who spiffed up everyone's shoes.

ow a public park, South Shore was then a private club with a large Irish Catholic membership and a pretty, tree-lined course on Lake Michigan, inside Chicago's city limits. It not only had a clubhouse, it had its own ornately furnished hotel, lots of red-clay tennis courts, a private beach and marina, and a bandshell for romantic summer dances under the stars. Dietrich always got us tee times in the thick of the action on Saturdays and Sundays. So there was

always a crowd on hand when we started our round, and the usual onslaught of first-tee jitters. Typically, Dietrich would put his ball down the middle, but short, and I would rattle mine among the alders on the righthand side. Then we would advance 20 paces to the ladies' tee. This was in the days before Linda had met and married Mike. Leslie's younger sister rounded out our foursome in those days. Linda was not as graceful a golfer as Leslie, but she cared more about scoring, and always kept her ball in play. Anyway, she would drive a respectable 185. Then there'd be a hush as Leslie, wearing her archaic smile, teed up her ball and let it rip with a swing that went at least 15 degrees past parallel. If she caught the ball just right, it would go 230 on the fly, and there'd be titters of enthusiasm from the gallery.

With all her pedigree, it was always surprising to me that Leslie did not give a hoot about golf. She never looked at the golf magazines I brought home or watched any of the tournaments on television. The subject of golf simply had no appeal. In her scheme of things, it was a trivial activity. It didn't even spark her curiosity when I came home smitten with my first visit to the Masters or the Open. Leslie was also congenitally unfit for the relaxed and sometimes superficial social settings of club life. Her mother had become the consummate clubwoman in Fort Worth, but Leslie could not make small talk if her life depended on it.

Before a round, Leslie never hit balls. Her idea of warming up was to collect three clubs—her 6-, 7-, and 8-iron—in her grasp and swing them to and fro a half dozen times.

(I still warm up her way.) Then she would step up on the first tee and unleash a magnificent drive.

Perhaps because golf had been imposed on her, summer after summer, as a child by a well-intentioned but authoritarian father, Leslie failed to see the possibilities for joy in her game, or even that it might have played a role in the spiritual quest that overtook her life. But the only times she concentrated on a golf course were when she played with her father. Then her actions became more focused and deliberate, and if she misplayed a shot, her face darkened. I could tell she was doing her best to play well for him. Without his presence, her mind wandered. She still made wonderful shots, but often they were the wrong shots for the situations. And when she made bad shots, she shrugged them off. Without Dietrich bearing witness, she lost interest in connecting the dots.

There are times when I envy my friends who live in the South and who can play golf virtually every day of the year. But then I remind myself of the virtues of an off-season. Winter gives us time to add up the larger score. Even for those for whom golf is a career, golf is only a tender fraction of the whole. Winter discourages the monomania golfers are prone to, keeps it to a passion, nothing more. To think upon the past is to disarm it.

After Dietrich died, Leslie and I divorced, and she put away her clubs. But the memory of the girl with the model golf swing, and the game that might have been, lingers on.

MEMORABILIA
The PGA of America's Collection

Writing in *Golfiana* magazine, James Nolan recalled a brief shining moment that only true golf collectors would probably appreciate. It happened in 1986, when the PGA World Golf Hall of Fame arranged for an exhibit of the game's major historic golf trophies.

For a short while, under one roof, there you had the trophies for the British Open, the U.S. Open, the Masters, the PGA Championship, the Ryder Cup, and the British Amateur; the prizes for the Hagen and Vardon awards; the Open Medal of 1872; and, last but not least, the 1860 Belt—the trophy given to Young Tom Morris for winning the Open three times in succession—1868, 1869, and 1870.

Ray Davis, who arranged that exhibit, was the first curator of the PGA's extensive collection, and an ardent collector himself. Caddieing as a kid at a course in Indiana in the 1920s, his first acquisitions were Scottish-made hickory-shafted clubs that a bad-tempered golfer of that day regularly tossed into the stream that wandered through the layout. A book the local librarian introduced him to—a dusty

From the PGA's extensive collections (OPPOSITE), a print of a wintry golf scene, a sterling silver martini set dating from the 1930s, and an upholstered English chair evoke a favorite pastime. The hat, worn by Bing Crosby during several editions of the legendary Crosby Pro Am, was donated when the golf-addicted entertainer was named to the PGA World Golf Hall of Fame. The silver match safes (ABOVE RIGHT), date from the 1890s, including one inscribed, "Porthcawl Spring Meeting, Winner Fred Milburn." The bronze (RIGHT) is an anonymous golfing figure.

A turn-of-the-century flask (RIGHT) of Gorham silver and a combination bottle opener and corkscrew from the 1930s attest to golf's traditions of celebration and conviviality.

copy of Horace G. Hutchinson's classic, *Golf*, from the Badminton Library of Sports series—instilled in Davis a curiosity about golf history and tradition that would govern a lifetime of collecting.

The man who succeeded Davis, Dick Stranahan, was also an avid collector. "From the time I was very young," Stranahan, a former touring pro and club professional, once recalled, "I had an appreciation for art and antiquities of all kinds. But my collecting days really started when I won a few things in competition and put them away." Then he and his wife, Bee, visited the R & A's museum in St. Andrews, and they both became hooked on collecting golf memorabilia. Many golfers can't afford the prices fetched today by rare golf books, ceramics, silver, and other desirable art and antiquities with a golf theme, but collections like that of the PGA, the USGA, and the R & A give the public a chance to savor the treasures first-hand.

Collecting, at its most worthy, is about saving, not hoarding. Herb Graffis, a pioneer in American golf publishing who founded *Golfdom*, once inscribed a book he gave to Ray Davis with a tribute to any authentic golf collector: "His genius makes yesterday alive today in golf."

A collection of over 15,000 golf balls (LEFT), most donated by Norman Hutter of Florida and Sam Stein of California, conveys the multifaceted, often antic world of golf in logos from "Kalamazoo Elks" to "Corrigan Funeral Homes," U.S. presidential seals, and messages like "It's Not Nice to Slice" and "Think Positive—Quit." The balls covered in coral were fetched from water hazards in Hawaii. Some 10,000 instruments for marking the scorecard (OPPOSITE) were amassed by Paul Rawden of Connecticut over a 10-year period as he traveled the world "in search of pars and pencils."

AGAWAM COUNTRY CLUB
Agawam

ALBEMARLE GOLF COURSE
West Newton

ALLENDALE C. C.
North Dartmouth

* ALLENDALE CC *
North Dartmouth

ALLENDALE COUNTRY CLUB
North Dartmouth

AMESBURY GOLF & C. C.
Amesbury

AMHERST GOLF CLUB
Amherst

ANDOVER COUNTRY CLUB
Andover

* ANDOVER COUNTRY CLUB *
Andover

ASHFIELD COMMUNITY GOLF CLUB
Fairfield

ASHFIELD GOLF CLUB
Ashfield

B&M PAR 3 & MIN. GOLF SPFLD.MA
Springfield

BAKERS MINIATURE GOLF
Lanesborough

BARRINGTON SCHOOL G.C.
Great Barrington

* BASS RIVER GOLF CLUB *
South Yarmouth

BASS RIVER G.C.
South Yarmouth

BASS RIVER GOLF COURSE
South Yarmouth

BASS RIVER GOLF COURSE
South Yarmouth

* BASS RIVER GOLF COURSE *
South Yarmouth

BASS ROCKS GOLF CLUB
Gloucester

BAYBERRY HILLS GOLF COURSE

BAYBERRY HILLS GOLF COURSE

BAY PATH GOLF CLUB

BAY POINTE C. C.
Wareham

* BEAR HILL GOLF CLUB *
Stoneham

* BEAR HILL GOLF CLUB *
Haydenville

BEAVER BROOK COUNTRY CLUB

BEDFORD COUNTRY CLUB
Bedford

BEDFORD V.A. HOSPITAL G.C.
Bedford

BELLEVUE GOLF CLUB
Melrose

BELMONT COUNTRY CLUB

BELMONT COUNTRY CLUB

BELMONT SPRING

CONCORD COUNTRY CLUB
Concord

TONY CONIGLIARO'S C.C.
Nahant

COMMONWEALTH COUNTRY CLUB
Brookline

COONEMESSETT COUNTRY CLUB
Hatchville

Cotuit Highground Golf Club
Cotuit

COTUIT HIGHGROUND G. C.
Cotuit

COTUIT HIGHGROUND G. C.
Cotuit

THE COUNTRY CLUB
Brookline

THE COUNTRY CLUB
Brookline

* THE COUNTRY CLUB *
Brookline

THE COUNTRY CLUB
Brookline

1882 TO 1982
Brookline

THE COUNTRY CLUB
East N...

THE C. C. EAST
Brookline

THE COUNTRY CLUB
Brookline

C. C. OF BILLERICA
Billerica

Country Club of Greenfield
Greenfield

COUNTRY CLUB OF GREENFIELD
Greenfield

The COUNTRY CLUB of NATICK
Natick

Country Club of New Bedford
New Bedford
Mashpee

* COUNTRY CLUB OF NEW SEABURY *
Green Course
Mashpee

* COUNTRY CLUB OF NEW SEABURY *
Blue Course-100
Mashpee

COUNTRY CLUB of NEW SEABURY
Green Challenger
Mashpee

COUNTRY CLUB of NEW SEABURY
Blue Champ Challen
Mashpee

* COUNTRY CLUB OF NEW SEABURY *
Blue Course
Mashpee

* COUNTRY CLUB OF NEW SEABURY *
Green Course

COUNTRY CLUB OF PITTSFIELD

CRANBERRY VALLEY GOLF COURSE

FO

F

FRANC

FR

FRAN

FU

GA

GARDNER

GEOR

GOLFLA

G

GREAT

COUNT

GRE

GREE

The copper-cupolaed Pinehurst Hotel (LEFT) is the center of a 126-hole golf resort that dates from 1895, when soda fountain tycoon James W. Tufts bought 10,000 acres of land in the Sandhills to develop as a health-oriented winter retreat. Tee markers (BELOW), now in the Tufts Archives, were used on one of the first courses built early in the century, as the curative powers of golf became the area's main draw.

Pinehurst's practice range, "Maniac Hill" (BELOW), beyond the fleet of golf carts, is only a few restless steps from five of the seven courses operated by the resort, of which No. 2 (OPPOSITE) is justly the most famous. When the original layout of the course was completed in 1907, it featured square sand greens.

ESCAPE
Golf in Pinehurst

The center of winter out-of-door life in the Middle South," the ad for Pinehurst proclaimed in 1911, "free from climatic extremes and wholesome in every respect." In that year the resort already offered the unheard-of luxury of three 18-hole golf courses, "all in pink of condition," and its reputation among serious golfers was growing in tandem with that of its resident golf architect, Donald Ross, and its annual golf tournament, the North and South Open, inaugurated in 1901. The richly furnished Carolina Hotel, "Queen of the South," had opened, and all season long, trains on the Seaboard line pulled in daily with their well-heeled, winter-weary passengers from the north.

Richard S. Tufts, grandson of Pinehurst founder James W. Tufts, credited Ross, Walter J. Travis, and Boston advertising man Frank Presbrey for Pinehurst's early success in his book, *The Scottish Invasion*.

Travis, who edited *The American Golfer*, the leading golf magazine of its day, from 1909 to 1920, spent part of many winters at Pinehurst, winning the North and South three times. The tacit imprimatur of this first American-made golf champion was important to the new golf facility.

Presbrey encouraged the Tufts family to conduct a host of golf tournaments, as competition was becoming increasingly popular with the growing number of newcomers to the game.

Pinehurst has survived a century of progress remarkably well, its traditions still intact in its village of curving roads and vintage cottages, and at the now 40-odd courses within a short driving distance of town.

A life-size bronze of Donald Ross (RIGHT) looks out over the finishing green of the architect's prize creation, Pinehurst No. 2 (ABOVE). A view of the 4th hole (OPPOSITE), a 547-yard par-5 from the back tees, reveals some of the subtle mounds, swales, and dips that make golf on and around a vintage Ross green an adventure. BELOW: A caddie on No. 2 waits for his golfer's putt to drop on the 5th hole.

The Art of Golf-Course Design

Michael J. Hurdzan's studio in Columbus, Ohio, is a workplace where the past meets the future in golf-course architecture. Drafting tables where golf holes are designed using the latest computer technology share space with a collection of golf antiquities that began in 1968, when someone gave Mike the book, *Golf Architecture in America,* by George Thomas. Hurdzan, who has designed over 200 golf courses over the past three decades, including the critically acclaimed Devil's Pulpit in Canada and Eagles Stick in Ohio, has been adding on ever since. "It's a sickness, it really is," he laughs. "Anything having to do with golf

The studio (BELOW) of a golf-course architect who is also a lifelong collector contains his own handiwork and the pre-computer visions of earlier designers of far-ranging influence, such as Stanley Thompson (ABOVE AND RIGHT).

interests me." He has accumulated some 3,000 books, many on golf-course design and maintenance, some 6,000 wood-shafted clubs, thousands of golf balls, and a smattering of everything else. Over the office copying machine are movie posters for those two golfing epics, *Follow the Sun* and *Caddyshack.* In the room where blueprints are spit out by an electrostatic plotting machine is a photograph of the founding members of the Society of Golf Course Architects of America. Someday, Hurdzan hopes to organize his collection in its own exhibit rooms at the studio, giving clients a taste of the traditions that the architect strives to bring to his work, "using the elements of strategic design that flourished in the 1920s." But for now, Glenn Ford and Bill Murray will be staring at anyone who uses the copier at Hurdzan Golf Course Design.

When golf architects, including Donald Ross, second from right (ABOVE), gathered at Pinehurst in 1948, it was not only to create a professional trade group but to discuss the fees the growing market might bear. Original drawings by Ross and other early expressions of a fledgling art (BELOW) are an integral part of Michael Hurdzan's collection. Views of Devil's Paintbrush (OVERLEAF), a Hurdzan design near Toronto, Canada.

One of the oldest clubs in Scotland, dating from 1780, Royal Aberdeen is a 6,372-yard, par-70 links that does not hand out its trophies lightly. Meandering between rolling farmland and the oil-rich North Sea, the layout has many deep bunkers, impenetrable gorse, and a number of blind shots.

RETURN TO SCOTLAND
Aberdeen and Blairgowrie

If winter condemns many golfers to forgo their favorite pastime, it also affords opportunity for reflection, and for planning the ultimate fantasy, a trip to where it all began.

The pilgrimage to Scotland begins in St. Andrews, and rightly so, but to sound the true depths of the Scottish golf tradition one must get about a bit. With the possible exception of the new traffic circles in Dundee, the country of Scotland—28,000 square miles—is easily navigable by car, and golf courses great and small are always within grasp, most of them accessible to visitors if arrangements are made in advance. It does not matter if the courses are heralded or obscure. And it takes only a couple of rounds with the natives, on their native grounds, to discover that all the myths and legends

An unmistakable Scottish mien inhabits the photographic roster of former captains of the club (OPPOSITE). The chair, presented by the captain for the 1870—71 term, is used only twice a year for meetings. Anyone caught sitting in it at any other time is obligated to buy a drink for everyone in the club.

ROYAL ABERDEEN

Captains of the Aberdeen Golf Club

The oldest surviving women's golf club in Scotland is the Aberdeen Ladies' Golf Club. Its clubhouse (BELOW AND RIGHT) contains a "suggestion book" with entries from 1894 "that each member should lend a book to form a library for the use of the club," and "that hairpins and hatpins be procurable from Mrs. Scott." On April 14, 1901, the suggestion "that a larger mirror be put in the club room" was immediately followed by another "that *no* mirror be put in the club room."

The feather golf ball or "feathery", was used for at least two and a half centuries, and was the product of highly skilled craftsmen. Both sides of a strip of ox belly-hide were stitched to the circumference of two circular pieces. The leather was turned inside out, soaked and placed in a cup shaped stand. Sufficient feathers, from the breast of a goose, to fill a top hat, were boiled in water and then stuffed into the the ball using a stuffing rod or brogue. The last seam was tightly stitched, during drying the leather contracted, and the feathery filling expanded to form a very solid ball.

Wishing you a Merry CHRISTMAS

Best Wishes

The "DRIVE"
Practice Golf

3
Maxfli

Feather Ball
circa. 1840

Ball Mould &
Bramble Colonel
circa. 1900

Tee Mould
circa. 1900

associated with the game in Scotland are true.

"The greatest experience in playing golf in Scotland," says Robert F. Kroeger in his introduction to the *Complete Guide to the Golf Courses of Scotland,* "is to play with a club member, share stories, and cap it off at the 19th hole in the members' club room, replete with ancient photos and golfing memorabilia." Although Kroeger is high on fraternization at clubs along the way in Scotland, he warns Americans who fall in with local golfers to pick up the pace, since most Scots like to play quickly.

The official birthplace of fast play in Scotland may well be Aberdeen. It is believed that the first five-minute rule for finding a lost ball was put into

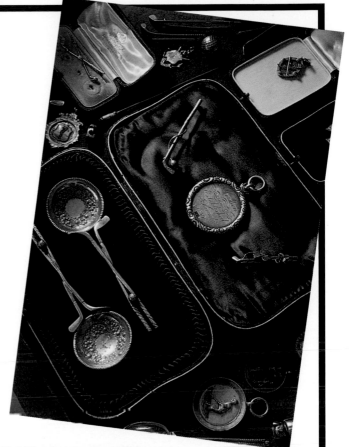

Aberdeen-related silver in the MacAskill collection (RIGHT) includes wine-tasting spoons once used by club captains at spring and autumn meeting dinners, and the oldest known junior golf medal in the world, dated 1839. The par-3 8th hole at Aberdeen (BELOW), 147 yards long, calls for a middle-iron to a green surrounded with 10 bunkers, as beautiful as it is challenging when the gorse is in flower in the spring.

In the former church (ABOVE) where Royal Aberdeen's golf professional Ronnie MacAskill lives and keeps his extensive collection, Edwardian hatpins and greeting cards oversee an instructive display case of old golf balls (OPPOSITE). The second ball from the left is a hand-hammered gutta-percha ball made by Allan Robertson in St. Andrews. It's of special interest because he was a feather-ball maker who feared the new material as a threat to his business. "Go and find them," he once told an assistant, referring to gutta-perchas, "and burn the filth."

writing here, in "Regulation 9 for Playing Golf in the Aberdeen Links," issued on October 7, 1815.

Esteem for speed, and also endurance, may also be detected in a document on exhibit in the clubhouse, dated June 27, 1908, attesting to "Mr. Harry B. Lumsden's Remarkable Feat." Lumsden, a member at Royal Aberdeen, "played 9 rounds over the old Balgownie Links averaging 82.2 strokes per round, starting at 5:15 A.M. and finishing at 8:30 P.M., with only the odd cup of Bovril and a little lime juice and water as sustenance. Mr. Lumsden covered approximately 35 miles."

While visiting Scotland, it would be a shame to overlook the country's many challenging inland

Most fairways and greens (LEFT) at Blairgowrie are individually sequestered in mature pine forest. Overlooking Rosemount's finishing hole, the clubhouse (BELOW) was built in 1939, replacing the more rustic "pavilions" that had existed, one for men, one for ladies. But within a month of the opening, with the outbreak of World War II, the new clubhouse was serving as barracks for a batallion of the Coldstream Guards.

courses. Although these parkland layouts are in sharp contrast to the windswept links along the coast, they offer the same depth of design and tradition. When Blairgowrie Golf Club opened in 1889, Old Tom Morris pronounced it "the most beautiful inland green I have ever seen." Located about an hour's drive due west of St. Andrews, in Perthshire, Blairgowrie boasts two 18-hole courses, plus the 9-hole Wee Course, a favorite of juniors and oldsters. Rosemount and Lansdowne, 6,581 yards and 6,865 yards respectively, wind through a forest of pine and ghosty silver birch on the former estate of the Marquis of Lansdowne. The layout of the Rosemount course, a frequent tournament site today, bears the hand of both James Baird, the five-time British Open winner, and Dr. Alister Mackenzie, Bobby Jones's esteemed collaborator at Augusta National.

Blairgowrie's 455 acres are home to pheasants, partridges, water hens, curlews, and many other bird species.

An early-morning view of Rosemount's 12th green (RIGHT). Scotsmen are loath to give up their golfing privileges (BELOW), so when walking the course becomes too strenuous, they are allowed the luxury of a "buggy"—provided they present proof of infirmity from their doctors to the club. Guest play at Blairgowrie accounts for about 12,000 rounds per year.

MASTER GOLF PROFESSIONAL
Lessons from Golf History

At some 50 practice stations stretching along one of the vast and verdant practice tees at the PGA National Golf Club, Palm Beach Gardens, Florida, little piles of white sand have been deposited, along with piles of range balls. Master teaching professional Dr. Gary Wiren is about to give over 100 golfers a clinic on sand play, and nothing has been left to chance.

Wiren, the former education director of the PGA of America, is one of the game's top teachers, traveling around the world to teach other teachers his "Laws, Principles, and Preferences" model that he says governs the golf swing. He is also a lecturer on golf history; an inventor of practice devices; an author of instructional books and videos, including the Official PGA Teaching Manual; and an inveterate collector of golf books, clubs, balls, trophies, and ephemera. He brings to everything his for-

Gary Wiren's eclectic golf collection does not overlook the humble tee, made of wood, plastic, or metal, including the Chicago-made Rex—25 cents for a packet of 18. Sheet music from the turn-of-the-century (ABOVE RIGHT) harks back to the era when the new game was something to sing about. Postcards from 1910s (RIGHT) extol the virtues of golf in humorous and even fold-out fashion.

Gary Wiren's club collection is organized to show the progression in size and design of equipment through the ages. Slender, wooden headed "long-nose" clubs were made from about 1450 to the late 1880s, the period when feather balls were used. After development of the gutta-percha ball around 1850, long, shallow-faced clubs gave way to a more compact head design. After Coburn Haskell invented the wound-rubber ball in Akron, Ohio, in 1898, it appeared on the market with a greater variety of surface patterns (OPPOSITE), each purporting to deliver more distance and accuracy.

midable organizational powers, a no-holds-barred insistence on quality, and, in matters of golf, a deep respect for the history and traditions of the game.

But Gary also has a wry sense of humor that surfaces unexpectedly, such as when he challenges a couple of friends to a nocturnal golf match, requiring participants keep their ears on the ball, or which shows up in some of the offbeat materials he has acquired in his years of collecting.

The exhibits in his library, fashioned by his own hand but with a professional curator's knack, instruct as well as entertain. Understanding as only a master teacher can the role of equipment in the evolution of the golf swing, Gary has arranged antique clubs and feather, gutta-percha, and rubber-wound balls in such a way that even the novice golfer receives an object lesson in golf history.

In Gary Wiren's library, notable antique clubs, matching those in the picture, include (LEFT, FROM TOP): a Mills "Z" model putter; a "Schenectady putter"; a driving cleek with the head made in St. Andrews by Horace Rawlins, the first U.S. Open winner; and a mashie with a perforated shaft patented in 1914 by Spalding and nicknamed "The Whistler." Early in the century, cigarette silks (ABOVE LEFT) targeted the collegiate market. OPPOSITE: When A. Stanley Iles of Hoylake, England, invented his "retrieving putter" in 1934, he made sure it passed muster with the R & A before marketing it.

DIRECTORY

GOLF MUSEUMS AND LIBRARIES

UNITED STATES

The American Golf Hall of Fame
Foxburg Country Club
Box 305, Harvey Road
Foxburg, PA 16036
(412) 659-3196

Clubs, balls, books, and artwork on exhibit in the picturesque clubhouse.

James River Country Club
1500 Country Club Road
Newport News, VA 23606
(805) 596-4772

The museum and library at this club contain one of the largest collections of old clubs in the world, including a brassie used by Bobby Jones in all his national championship victories, from the 1925 British Open through the 1930 U.S. Amateur.

Jude E. Poynter Golf Museum
College of the Desert
43-500 Monterey Avenue
Palm Desert, CA 92260
(619) 341-2491

Golf antiques and memorabilia.

Ouimet Room
Massachusetts Golf Association
190 Park Road
Weston, MA 02193
(617) 891-4300

Collection devoted to the amateur career of Francis Ouimet and other New England golf notables.

PGA World Golf Hall of Fame
c/o Professional Golfers' Association of America
100 Avenue of the Champions
Palm Beach Gardens, FL 33418
(407) 624-8400

Contains numerous exhibits of clubs, balls, books, artwork, and memorabilia. (At the time of publication, this collection was scheduled to be moved to PGA headquarters in Florida.)

Pinehurst Resort and Country Club
P.O. Box 4000
Carolina Vista
Pinehurst, NC 28374
(800) 927-4653

The clubhouse, grill room, and bar have exhibits of tournament photographs and other early golfing artifacts of Pinehurst.

IN MEMORY OF "TOMMY"

The Ralph Miller Golf Library and Museum
One Industry Hills Parkway
City of Industry, CA 91744
(818) 854-2354

Excellent research library with some 6,000 golf titles.

Tufts Archives
Given Memorial Library
Village Green East Road
P.O. Box 159
Pinehurst, NC 28374
(919) 295-3642

Exhibits, books, correspondence, and other materials pertaining to the development of Pinehurst as a golf resort under several generations of the Tufts family.

U. S. Golf Association Museum and Library
P.O. Box 708
Liberty Corner Road
Far Hills, NJ 07931
(908) 234-2300

An impressive collection that includes 8,000 books, clubs and balls that trace the game's evolution, paintings, sculpture, ceramics, glassware, and silver.

CANADA

British Columbia Golf House Society
2545 Blanca Street
Vancouver, British
  Columbia
Canada V6R 4N1

Numerous golf exhibits including a "Golf Widow's Parlour," early club-making displays, and a 1,200-volume library.
(604) 943-4998

Canadian Golf Hall of Fame, Library, and Museum
Glen Abbey Golf Club
RR No. 2
1333 Dorval Drive
Oakville, Ontario
Canada L6J 423
(416) 849-9700

Collection owned and operated by the Royal Canadian Golf Association includes books, clubs, and trophies shedding light on Canadian golf history.

Canadian Golf Museum and Historical Institute
Kingsway Park Golf and
  Country Club
1461 Mountain Road
RR No. 2
Aylmer E., Quebec
Canada J9H 5E1
(819) 827-4403

Exhibit includes a collection of balls and clubs, books, and art.

SCOTLAND

British Golf Museum
Bruce Embankment
St. Andrews, Fife
Scotland KY16 9AB
0334 78880

Opposite the R & A, this museum opened in 1990

with both traditional exhibits and innovative multimedia exhibits that permit lively visitor participation.

The Heritage of Golf Museum
Gullane, East Lothian
Scotland
087 57 277

Located next to the first tee at the seaside links of Gullane, this small but delightful exhibit—the creation of golf historian and collector Archie Baird—covers golf "from the time when only a few people here in the East of Scotland coaxed their 'featheries' round the rough links, to the present day when multitudes of men and women spend vast fortunes on this pastime of beauty and skill." By appointment only.

DEALERS IN GOLF ANTIQUES AND COLLECTIBLES
Many of these dealers are available by appointment only.

CALIFORNIA

Cambridge Golf Antiquities
James Santy
The Lodge at Pebble Beach
P.O. Box 965
Pebble Beach, CA 95933
(408) 626-3334

Golf memorabilia, including antique and classic clubs, golf balls, sterling, glassware, bronzes, prints, and books. The Ray Davis Museum, benefiting junior golf, is a permanent exhibit.

Golf Art and Imports
P.O. Box 6208
Dolores at 6th Street
Carmel, CA 93921
(408) 625-4488

Golf gifts, art, and collectibles.

Maxwell's Bookmark
2103 Pacific Avenue
Stockton, CA 95204
(209) 466-0194

New, used, and out-of-print books.

CONNECTICUT

Paul Rawden
217 Alden Avenue
New Haven, CT 06519
(203) 387-1817

Golf pencils, scorecards, ball markers, and divot tools.

GEORGIA

Golf Collectibles, Ltd.
Henry Alperin
1450 Winter Street
Augusta, GA 30904
(706) 736-6626

Wood-shafted clubs.

Old Sport Golf
Bob Burkett
4297 N.E. Expressway
  Access Road
Doraville, GA 30340
(404) 493-4344

New and used golf clubs.

ILLINOIS

Old Chicago Golf Shop
Leo M. Kelly, Jr.
6244 Buchwood Road
Matteson, IL 60443
(708) 720-0046

Prints, books, wood-shafted clubs, other collectibles.

KENTUCKY

Mason's Golf Shop
Phillip Mason
403 Stringtown Road
Williamsburg, KY 40769
(606) 549-4827

Golf books and videos.

MASSACHUSETTS

Howard S. Mott, Inc.
Rusty Mott
P. O. Box 309
Sheffield, MA 01257
(413) 229-2019

Books and art.

NEW JERSEY

Rare Stuff
35 Woodward Road
Englishtown, NJ 07726
(201) 431-2585

Antique and classic clubs, golf balls, books, and prints.

NEW YORK

George Lewis/ Golfiana
P.O. Box 291
Mamaroneck, NY 10543
(914) 698-4579

Old books and decorative golf antiques.

Larry Lawrence Rare Sports
P.O. Box 756
Planetarium Station
New York, NY 10024
(212) 255-9230

Books and tournament programs.

Ray Hart
311 E. 240th Street
Bronx, NY 10470
(212) 324-5516
Golf collectibles.

Rare Books Limited
Eldon P. Steeves
P.O. Box 188
Colvin Station
Syracuse, NY 13205

Rare and old golf books.

Richard E. Donovan Enterprises
305 Massachusetts Avenue
P.O. Box 7070
Endicott, NY 13760
(607) 785-5874

Rare, out-of-print, and new golf books.

OHIO

Antiques & Golf Memorabilia
Greg and Barbara Hall
24717 East Oakland Road
Bay Village, OH 44140
(216) 871-9319

All types of golf collectibles.

North Berwick Golf Course

THIS IS A

CHILDRENS GOLF COURSE
NOT A PRACTICE AREA

All Dogs must be kept on a Lead

Old Golf Shop, Ltd.
325 W. Fifth Street
Cincinnati, OH 45202
(513) 241-7797

High-grade golf antiques
and art.

Table Rock Golf Club
Jim and Kathy Butler
3005 Wilson Road
Centerburg, OH 43011
(614) 965-3322

Classic clubs.

The Wooden Putter
1441 Grandview Avenue
Columbus, OH 43212
(614) 488-7888

Golf gifts, art, and antiques.

TEXAS

Crow & Co.
Antique Pavilion
2311 Westheimer Road
Houston, TX 77098
(713) 520-9755

Unique sporting antiques
including some golf.

Magnolia Station
Johnny R. Henry
Box 776
201 S. Dallas
Ennis, TX 75120
(214) 875-7360

Wood-shafted clubs and
other collectibles.

The Sporting Scene
2944 Congressman Lane
Dallas, TX 75220
(214) 350-6131

Golf art, trophies, and
other memorabilia.

VIRGINIA

American Golf Classics
12842 Jefferson Avenue
Newport News, VA 23602
(804) 874-7271

Classic clubs and golf
antiques.

WASHINGTON

**Golf Classics &
Collectibles**
Jeff Ellis
Box 843
1093½ Pioneer Way, No. 2
Oak Harbor, WA 928277
(206) 675-7611

Old and classic clubs.

CANADA

Golf Gap
3435 Yonge St.
Toronto, Ontario
Canada M4N 2N1
(416) 485-5316

Art, books, videos, and
gifts.

Jack Rutherford
P.O. Box 55
Pefferlaw, Ontario
Canada L0E 1N0
(705) 437-GOLF

Golf collectibles.

SCOTLAND

Auchterlonies
2 Golf Place
St. Andrews, Fife
Scotland KY16 9GA
0334 73253

Hand-crafted golf clubs and
"everything for the discern-
ing golfer."

J. C. Furniss
Crossway House
Torthorwald, Dumfries
Scotland DG1 3PT

Books, postcards, cigarette
cards.

**Old St. Andrews
Gallery**
9 Albany Place
St. Andrews, Fife
Scotland, KY16 9H4

Golf memorabilia and gifts.

Old Troon Sporting Antiques

49 Ayr Street
Troon, Ayrshire
Scotland KA10 6EB

Paintings, prints, and miscellaneous golf items.

Quarto Bookshop

8 Golf Place
St. Andrews, Fife
Scotland, KY16 9JA
0334 74616

New and used golf books

Rhod McEwan

Glengarden
Ballater, Aberdeenshire
Scotland AB35 5UB

Golf books.

St. Andrews Woolen Mill

The Golf Links
St. Andrews, Fife
Scotland KY16 9BR
0334 72366

Aisles and aisles of golf apparel and gifts.

Tom Morris Golf Shop

8 The Links
St. Andrews, Fife
Scotland KY16 9JB
0334 73499

Wide variety of golf merchandise.

ENGLAND

Burlington Gallery Ltd.

10 Burlington Gardens
London
England W1X 1LG

Prints, paintings, and ceramics.

The Crypt

Manfred Schotten
109 High Street
Burford, Oxfordshire
England OX18 4RG
0993 822302

Sporting antiquities including golf.

Golf Interest

P.O. Box 1226
East Sussex
England BN20 9DH

Clubs and miscellaneous golf items.

Grant Books

Victoria Square
Droitwich, Worcestershire
England WR9 8DE

Old, out-of-print, and new golf books and old clubs, artwork, and memorabilia.

FRANCE

Brandicourt

54, Avenue Victor Hugo
75116 Paris
France
45 00 76 16
Golf and other sporting antiquities.

MAJOR GOLF AUCTION HOUSES

UNITED STATES

Christie's

502 Park Avenue
New York, NY 10022
(212) 546-1000‹

Kevin McGrath Sporting Antiquities

P.O. Box 1386
47 Leonard Road
Melrose, MA 02176
(617) 662-6588

Oliver's Auction Gallery

Box 337
Route 1, Plaza 1
Kennebunk, ME 04043
(207) 985-3600

Phillips

406 East 79th Street
New York, NY 10021
(212) 570-4830

Sotheby's

1334 York Avenue
New York, NY 10021
(212) 606-7000

SCOTLAND

Christie's

164-166 Bath Street
Glasgow
Scotland G2 4TG

ENGLAND

Phillips
New House
150 Christleton Road
Chester, Cheshire
England CH3 5TD

Sotheby's
34/35 New Bond Street
London
England W1A 2AA

OTHER RESOURCES FOR COLLECTORS

Complete Guide to the Golf Courses of Scotland
By Robert Kroeger
Heritage Communications, 1992, 258 pages, $19.95
Distributed by Seven Hills Books
49 Central Avenue
Cincinnati, OH 45202
(513) 381-3881

A useful guide for planning a golf trip to Scotland, this book contains detailed descriptions of some 430 Scottish golf courses, with advice on how to obtain permission to play them (usually by writing in advance for permission)

and with reports on historic golf collections, large and small, encountered along the way.

The Encyclopedia of Golf Collectibles
By John M. Olman and Morton W. Olman
Books Americana, 1985, 304 pages, $20
Distributed by the Golf Shop Collection
P.O. Box 14609
Cincinnati, OH 45250
(513) 241-7789

A comprehensive guide to golf antiques and collectibles, lavishly illustrated and including approximate values and price ranges, covering balls, clubs, prints and paintings, ceramics, silver, bronzes and other statuary, books, periodicals, photographs, postage

stamps, cigarette cards, and other collectibles.

Golf Collectors' Society
P.O. Box 491
Shawnee Mission, KS 66201
(913) 649-4618

Founded in 1970 by J. Robert Kuntz and Joseph S. F. Murdoch, along with 25 charter members, this organization now has more than 2,000 members in a dozen countries, an international fraternity of "craftspeople, physicians, lawyers, curators or librarians of the world-class organizations we support, engineers, golf pros, salespeople, writers, architects, artists, or retired folk, (and) they all love the 'Gamye.'" The GCS publishes a bulletin and membership directory,

holds an annual fall meeting, and sponsors the Hickory Hacker Open with players dressed in period garb and swinging pre-1930 wood-shafted clubs.

Golfiana
Charles A. "Bud" Dufner, Editor
P.O. Box 668
Edwardsville, IL 62025
(618) 656-8172

A quarterly magazine, published by a longtime member of the Golf Collectors' Society, devoted to history, heritage, and arcane legacies of the game.

Golf Links
Louis S. DeLuca, Editor
5486 Georgetown Road
Frankfort, KY 40601
(502) 695-1035

A quarterly newsletter that publishes detailed contemporary accounts of visits to historic golfing regions, and also resurrects literary and instructional gems from golf's past.

Harvey Penick's Little Red Golf Letter
Harvey Penick, Editor Emeritus
Tinsley Penick, Editor-in-Chief
75 Holly Lane
Greenwich, CT 06836
(800) 424-7887

Monthly newsletter with reports on instruction, equipment, and travel from the point of view of a tradition-minded teacher of the game.

INDEX